THE
UNTOLD
STORY
OF THE
COMPUTER
REVOLUTION

THE
UNTOLD
STORY
OF THE
COMPUTER
REVOLUTION

Bits, Bytes, Bauds, and Brains

G. Harry Stine

ARBOR HOUSE
New York

Manufactured in the United States of America

10 9 8 7 6 5 4 3 2 1

This book is printed on acid free paper. The paper in this book meets the guidelines for permanence and durability of the Committee on Production Guidelines for Book Longevity of the Council on Library Resources.

Library of Congress Cataloging in Publication Data

Stine, G. Harry (George Harry), 1928-
 The untold story of the computer revolution.

 1. Computers. I. Title.
QA76.S833   1985   001.64   84-16736
ISBN: 0-87795-574-3 (alk. paper)

To
J. E. Pournelle, Ph.D.

CONTENTS

Introduction   9

1.   Deus ex Machina   13

2.   The Babbage Legacy   20

3.   The Dawn of the Computer Age   28

4.   The First Computer Companies   39

5.   The Business of Business Machines   47

6.   Dawn Over Silicon Valley   58

7.   Ballistics, Bombsights, and Brass Brains   67

8.   "Men, Minutes, Money"   79

9.   The Electrons Take Over   90

10.   The Vacuum Tube Monsters   102

11.   Computers Go Solid   129

12.   The False Dawn   140

13.   How Creative Was the Valley?   150

14.   Working on the Edge of Disaster   160

15.   Computer in Your Pocket   172

16.   The Computer Becomes Personal   182

17.   The Computer Becomes Competitive   193

18.   Boom, Bust, Shake-out, and "Excelsior!"   205

Epilogue   217

Photographs follow page   112

Introduction

T hough most people believe the computer revolution began a few years ago when they first heard about computers, or on that morning when they came into the office and found one there, it really started long before any reader of this book was born. And, actually, it isn't a revolution at all; rather it is more of an evolution. Because there is no system to accurately assess the long-term trends of civilization, let alone a single culture, historical accounts display a distorted perception of "revolution."

Although every revolution has a beginning and an end, and must be completed at some definite point in time, with the result being a new way of doing something or of thinking about things, there is no end in sight to the computer revolution. Maybe our perspective is too limited. Maybe we can't see what's happening because we're in the middle of it. Perhaps it's because evolutionary changes used to happen over centuries, and now they become apparent within a single lifetime.

But regardless of our understanding of the word *revolution,* the computer *has* changed our lives. And the complete story of how this happened has never been told. Nor will I tell it, because it would require volumes. Instead of including every anecdote and technical or business development, I've tried to explain patterns and trends that may help you get a clearer picture of the current state of the industry, as well as its future.

I had a lot of help, and it came quickly and readily from individuals in the computer industry who responded to my requests: Amy Arutt (Tandy Radio Shack); Carol E. Brewis

(Burroughs Corp.); Gene Carter (Apple Computer Co.); Joseph Ciasullo (Sperry Univac); Norman D. Clark (Bytronix Corp.); Susan Merz Cook (Four-Phase Systems, Inc.); John F. Cunningham (Wang Laboratories, Inc.); George De Benedetto (Lanier Business Products, Inc.); Michael Dickey (Cray Research, Inc.); Richard R. Douglas (Honeywell, Inc.); Terry A. Freeman (Vector Graphic, Inc.); Michael F. Klatman (Data General Corp.); R. K. Kramer (NCR Corp.); Peter E. McGuirk (Microdata Corp.); M. E. Price (Control Data Corp.); John Reese (Coleco Industries, Inc.); Barbara van Fleet (Honeywell, Inc.); Lane Webster (Hewlett-Packard Co.); and W. E. Whalley (IBM). Special thanks to my good friend and fellow author Frank Vaughn (Intel Corp.), who provided more data than I could absorb and more leads than I could follow up.

This book was written on a Vector Graphic System B using the Vector Graphic Word Processing System, Version 2.3, and it was printed on a Qume Sprint 5 letter-quality daisy-wheel printer.

—G. Harry Stine
Phoenix, Arizona

THE
UNTOLD
STORY
OF THE
COMPUTER
REVOLUTION

1

Deus ex Machina

Computers seem to be taking over, not only in America, Europe, and Japan, but everywhere in the world. Tasks formerly done by hundreds of people with desk calculators and pads of columnar paper are now done by computers that do the same jobs faster and are limited only by the human beings who program them and feed them data.

Will we all end up staring at the glowing screens of terminals while computers run the world?

Not likely.

This fear was born over a hundred years ago in the minds of a few romantic intellectuals and was picked up by others who never understood technology and thus feared the machine. In the utopian novel *Erewhon* (*nowhere* spelled backward), written by English satirist Samuel Butler in 1872, the setting was a land without machinery of any kind, a nineteenth-century "small is beautiful" and "back to nature" place. Echoing the science-out-of-control concept of Mary Wollstonecraft Shelley's 1818 novel *Frankenstein,* Butler wrote in *Erewhon:* "Are we not ourselves creating our successors . . . daily giving them greater skill and supplying more and more of that self-regulating, self-acting power which will be better than any intellect?" Butler, unlike inventors and scientists, seemed to have doubts about the capacity of the human intellect and worried about being replaced by machines.

People of action paid little or no attention to such intellectuals. Instead, they developed and put to use the technical tools that have relieved people of back-breaking and mind-shattering labor. By so doing, they've improved the human condition while at the same time learning more about who and what we are.

Just as machinery has supplanted and increased human and animal muscle power, so the modern-day digital computer in all its many forms has been developed over many decades as a tool to extend the human mind and, like any other tool, will never become a master unless people permit it to. And is it likely that the human race, having spent millions of years taking control of this planet, will succumb now? We are certainly smart enough not to create our own competition!

A tool is always invented to make possible something that was formerly impossible—or extremely difficult. The evolution of the computer over the last 150 years has occurred to serve such a purpose. Developed in response to a growing number of urgent social needs, the computer was desperately needed as a tool to help people manage a rapidly increasing volume of information. The factor behind the development of information-handling machines we now call computers was economics.

Understanding this background will be helpful in gaining some perspective on the computer's role in our daily lives, and on what the future may hold for people and computers.

In the past 250 years, human life and society has undergone a profound change, perhaps the greatest since the dawn of the Neolithic Age some ten thousand years ago, when the majority of the few people on the earth gave up nomadic hunting for farming. The late Herman Kahn called this "the Great Transition." It isn't discontinuous with the trends of historical development, but a long-term trend, and there is no basis for believing it will reverse itself.

Recently, some twentieth-century romantics have tried to convince people that there are limits to everything by pointing toward the inevitable, unimaginable evil of progress; they say that human beings are a cancer in the earth's environment and that change should be stopped in favor of a return to the good old days, a simpler life of "low tech" and "decentralized technology." This story didn't sell a century ago, and it doesn't sell today either.

In 1980, we "rediscovered" progress. During the anti-technology period, the computer as we know it today was perfected. The modern digital computer, obviously, isn't the cause of the Great Transition. It's an invention made by human beings trying to cope with the enormous number of changes going on around us all the time at an ever-increasing rate, the result of the continuous amassing of new information and data.

The rapid and massive changes of the Great Transition are historically new to human experience. Pulitzer prize winner Daniel J. Boorstin, in his book *The Exploring Spirit,* points out that until a few centuries ago people lived in an age of again-and-again: looking to the golden age of the past for guidance, they felt nothing would be different in the future. The sun rose and set every day. The seasons came in sequence. Occasionally, catastrophes of weather, climate, or geology would devastate the status quo. Invaders would arrive over the hills, loot and rape, depose the existing rulers, be assimilated, and in turn be conquered by the next wave of invaders. Peasants toiled, suffered, and died early. Merchants traded and bartered. If life was short and brutal, it was at least understood that there were few surprises. You could always look back at what your parents had experienced and expect the same. In this comfort of the known, the unknown was feared. And to a great extent, this is still true, even in the minds of many Americans.

Though we may be aware of the Great Transition and we manage to work with many of the changes taking place, most of us are still shocked by its magnitude, speed, and variety.

It's amazing to note that ninety percent of the scientists who *ever* lived are now alive, continually discovering new information. At this moment, new data (information) is being generated, created, and discovered at the rate of ten pages of single-spaced typewritten copy every minute of every hour of every day. Over forty thousand new book titles are published every year in the United States alone.

The total amount of knowledge, data, and information possessed by the human race is doubling every seven years.

In the next thirty-day period, the following changes will occur:

- 5,991 new patents will be granted.
- 1,987 new trademarks will be registered.

- 670 new products will be announced.
- 26,620 new businesses will be incorporated.
- 1,080 existing businesses will close their doors.
- 84 companies will disappear through merger.

According to the telephone companies (AT&T, GTE, or the new regional firms, although they're changing, too), in the next twelve-month period, any community in the United States will experience a 30 percent change based on the installation of new, disconnected, or moved telephones.

Dun and Bradstreet, the credit-rating company, makes more than ten thousand changes *per week* in its data base.

One of the most valuable commercial data bases in the United States is Thomas Register. It lists and categorizes all U.S. commercial firms in terms of products or services produced. It includes the presidents, sales contacts, office and plant addresses, and telephone numbers of all these firms. It is important to have the latest edition because Thomas Register now incorporates more than a million changes per year.

Next year, the numbers will be different. They will be greater.

Not only have we faced a problem of how to classify, store, locate, and recover all the information we have and are generating, but we have had a problem of evaluating it once we had it in hand. What does it all mean? Are there any correlations or relationships between seemingly diverse bits of data?

Insurance companies began to flourish because businessmen and investors demanded insurance as a means to reduce the risks inherent in doing business. Establishing underwriting guidelines wasn't just a problem for life insurance companies, which had to develop accurate actuarial tables or go out of business; it was a data-management problem for *all* types of insurance firms. Statistical manipulation of the mountains of data required acres of people—and it threatened to bury them.

Back in 1960, the New York Stock Exchange (NYSE) had a record day with a total volume of four million shares traded. In early 1984, an ordinary day on Wall Street saw about eighty million shares change hands on a day with "moderate trading volume."

It used to require thousands of people to keep track of the transactions of the NYSE, where it was absolutely necessary to know who bought or sold what and who owned it. That is not even to mention the transactions of the American Stock Exchange, Over-the-Counter exchange (OTC), National Association of Securities Dealers Automated Quotations (NASDAC), precious metals, grain markets, or futures markets, the Paris Bourse, and the other stock exchanges elsewhere in the world. The pressures of business expansion brought about by both reinvestment of capital wealth and technical development of new products and services posed an overwhelming problem in data management. Not only has the volume of the NYSE increased by a factor of more than ten in a quarter of a century, but the number of firms listed has also increased. Many of the new corporations now listed are those that have been responsible for making the change possible. But what created what? Did the problem's solution create more problems? Yes, but in a way few people recognize.

It was patently obvious as long ago as 1890 that we had a serious problem with data processing. Millions of people would have to be involved in nothing more than reading, logging, filing, retrieving, copying, and transporting information. Humanity was drowning in a rising ocean of paper. And it soon would be facing a real limits-to-growth future because of this inability to handle the data and information that we were generating and using. We would become a species of paper shufflers. Indeed, in a majority of the world that *is* the case.

Enormous bureaucracies have grown up in order to cope with the problems of information handling in social organizations. The "in" and "out" baskets are symptoms of unprogressive institutional policies for information handling.

And if a bureaucracy such as the United States government is going to handle the taxation, medical, and retirement affairs of large numbers of people, it's got to have a census and know how many people are where doing what. When the Roosevelt administration brought into existence the original American welfare state in the 1930s, such bureaucracies as the Social Security Administration suddenly found themselves with a huge data-management task. Such data-management demands by big, centralized governments caused them to be among the first advocates of the computer industry.

There had to be an answer to the data-management problem. There had to be a basic tool that made the answer feasible.

The solution, the new computer tool, would both facilitate and create new social institutions in the process of helping to solve the problem.

Naturally, technology creates new problems as it goes about solving old ones. But the problems could be solved more rapidly now; and we created new social institutions to control the technologies.

The *deus ex machina** of today's world is the electronic digital computer in all its forms. It answers the problem of handling data because it's a very fast adding machine.

A group of bright people did not just sit down and "invent" the computer as a solution to the problems of the information explosion. It took years of technical progress to make some computer feats possible. But it also took a growing realization that data could be translated into a form acceptable to these fast adding machines. And that data in turn was data.

The conversion of the computing machine to an information-management tool is really what's been going on for the past two decades. It's what's behind the "computer revolution."

In North America, Western Europe, and Japan, the information-processing machine we call a computer has just started to revolutionize not only our homes, offices, schools, cars, appliances, and tools, but also the way we think—because we've learned something about *how* we think in the process of developing this new tool.

The computer has also drastically altered our economic system. It has not only *helped* cope with change, but has *made possible* entirely new organizations, such as new kinds of companies and corporations. The speed with which the computer took over as a major information processor is remarkable.

Over the past sixty years, there's been only *one* company remotely connected with computers (and no longer directly connected with them) that's remained on Forbes' annual list of the top 100 corporations in the United States: General Electric.

In 1917 it was the only such company listed in the top 100 by Forbes.

---

*Literally, "god from the machine." From an ancient Greek theatrical device, whereby a god was lowered via a derrick from "heaven" to solve the problem of the play.

In 1929, GE was joined on the list by RCA, but that was primarily because of radio.

In 1945, International Business Machines (IBM) appeared on the list for the first time. It was number 64.

By 1966, the computer revolution had just started. Eight firms making computers appear on the Forbes list: GE (9), IBM (10), GTE (11), ITT (22), RCA (39), Sperry-Rand (60), and Honeywell (88). A runner-up was NCR (117).

In 1977, Burroughs joined the list.

All of the personal computer companies (except IBM) have emerged since 1945. Companies such as Motorola and Texas Instruments, which were originally created to do something else, have moved strongly into the microelectronics and computer markets. Intel, Data General, Digital, Control Data, Commodore, Coleco, General Data, Apple, Vector Graphic, and others that are creations of the computer age weren't even listed on the various stock exchanges in 1970!

And growth is still occurring. But now we've got an intellectual tool to help us cope with it. We've got a *real* god in a machine.

2

The Babbage Legacy

Although most people believe the computer is a twentieth-century development, its roots go back centuries. To truly understand the computer revolution, we must not only know where the computer is today, but we must trace its origins.

The basic principles of the modern computer were worked out between the years 1813 and 1833. At this time there was a dire need to process information faster and more accurately in the form of tables of mathematical functions.

Today, we hardly think about it when we go to a reference book for a table of numbers. A modern scientist, engineer, financier, insurance underwriter, or statistician isn't required to spend hours with a pen and pencil, laboriously calculating multiplications, logarithms, powers, trigonometric functions, amortization, life expectancy, or standard deviation. If he or she has any sort of modern digital microcomputer capable of running the ubiquitous BASIC program, the computer will calculate the desired numbers using internal programming. If the computer is connected to a good data base, it will find those tables in its memory. Even if a person doesn't yet have a computer, he or she simply can look up the required table in a reference volume such as *Mark's Mechanical Engineer's Handbook, The Handbook of Chemistry and Physics,* or any little mathematics handbook of precalculated numbers.

It's hard to believe that three hundred years ago even the most highly educated people in the world could hardly manage anything more complicated than their two-times multiplication tables. The need for calculating machines was obvious. The German mathematician Baron Gottfried Wilhelm von Leibnitz (1646-1716) said: "It is unworthy of excellent men to lose hours like slaves in the labor of calculation which could be safely relegated to anyone if machines were used."

But it was an English mathematician who came up with the basic principles upon which the modern computer is based. As a child in Somerset, Charles Babbage (1792-1871) was tutored at home because of ill health. By the time he got to Trinity College, he was far ahead of his teachers in mathematics. He became a member of the Analytical Society formed by John Herschel and George Peacock. The members promised each other to "do their best to leave the world wiser than they found it."

In his memoirs, Charles Babbage wrote:

> The earliest idea that I can trace in my own mind of calculating arithmetical Tables by machinery arose in this manner:—
>
> One evening I was sitting in the rooms of the Analytical Society, at Cambridge, my head leaning forward on the table in a kind of dreamy mood, with a Table of logarithms lying open before me. Another member, coming into the room, and seeing me half asleep, called out, "Well, Babbage, what are you dreaming about?" to which I replied, "I am thinking that all these Tables (pointing to the logarithms) might be calculated by machinery."
>
> . . . About 1819 I was occupied with devising means for accurately dividing astronomical instruments, and had arrived at a plan which I thought was likely to succeed perfectly. I had also at that time been speculating about making machinery to compute arithmetical Tables.
>
> One morning I called upon the late Dr. Wollaston, to consult him about my plan for dividing instruments. On talking over the matter, it turned out that my system was exactly that which had been described by the Duke de Chaulines, in the Memoirs of the French Academy of

Sciences, about fifty or sixty years before. I then mentioned my other idea of computing Tables by machinery, which Dr. Wollaston thought a more promising subject.

I considered that a machine to execute the mere isolated operations of arithmetic, would be comparatively of little value, unless it were very easily set to do its work, and unless it executed not only accurately, but with great rapidity, whatever it was required to do.

But Babbage had grander ideas. He wanted to build a general-purpose machine, or "analytical engine," capable of performing any mathematical operation. In about 1833, he purchased a house on a quarter acre of ground and converted the coach house into a forge and foundry and the stables into a workshop. There he began the design and construction of a mechanical analytical engine.

According to Babbage, an analytical engine had to consist of two parts:

1. The store in which all the variables to be operated upon, as well as those quantities which have arisen from the result of other operations, are placed.

2. The mill in which the quantities about to be operated upon are always brought.

In modern terms what Babbage was describing would be called a computer memory ("store") and a central processing unit or CPU (the "mill").

His analytical engine would contain:

1. Apparatus for printing on paper, one, or, if required, two copies of the results.

2. Means for producing a stereotype mould of the tables or the results it computes.

3. Mechanism for punching on blank pasteboard cards or metal plates the numerical results of any of its computations.

Here Babbage is talking about what we call "input-output (I/O) peripherals," mechanisms for putting data into a computer and for allowing the computer to report its output or results.

But in 1833, Babbage didn't have electronics. He didn't even have electricity. Nobody did. Electricity was fifty years in the future, and electronics a century away. So, like all engineers, technologists, and inventors, Babbage was constrained by the technology of the time: he had steam power, mechanical actions, levers, gears, cams, and other mechanical motions. Thus, the speed of his analytical engine was excruciatingly slow by today's standards, although it had the capacity to do much more.

The Analytical Engine I propose will have the power of expressing every number it uses to fifty places or figures. It will multiply any two such numbers together, and then, if required, will divide the product of one hundred figures by a number of fifty place figures.

Supposing the velocity of the moving parts of the Engine to be not greater than forty feet per minute, I have no doubt that:

Sixty additions or subtractions may be completed and printed in one minute.

One multiplication of two numbers, each of fifty figures, in one minute.

One division of a number having one hundred places of figures by another of fifty in one minute.

A hand calculator won't handle fifty-digit numbers today. Neither will most personal computers. In most cases, eight-place numbers suffice when dealing with most of the real world around us. However, a $9.95 pocket calculator will handle those eight-digit numbers so fast that, as far as the human operator is concerned, it's instantaneous.

If Babbage had been able to complete his steam-powered analytical engine, it would have followed the instructions programmed into it by its human operators. It would have been capable of making decisions about which operation to follow next, based upon the results of its own work. Information would have been entered into it on punch cards. Both information and instructions would have been stored in a memory. The machine would have followed instructions from the operation punch cards. The processing unit would have performed operations on the information and returned the results to the memory. The final results would have been printed out or automatically set in type. It would have stored a thousand fifty-digit numbers in its memory. When it needed additional values for the calculation in progress, it would have signaled its human operators by ringing a bell.

The Babbage analytical engine might have been an impressive device to watch, with its huge cams and gears and wheels whirring and clanking. (Like a Watt steam engine, machinery of that period was noisy, full of the "monkey motion" of mechanical movements.) But Babbage never completed his analytical engine. It was far too complex and technologically ahead of its time. The accuracy he demanded was beyond the capabilities of mid-nineteenth century technology. The gears, linkages, and cams were not up to the job.

Babbage's work lay neglected for more than three-quarters of a century.

Why?

Just as many inventors were born too soon, so are many inventions. Sometimes the technology simply isn't up to the task demanded by the basic principles of the invention. But usually it's because there is no human desire for the invention. Therefore, it has no market, which is another way of saying that it has little or no perceived value to people.

In the case of the Babbage analytical engine, it was a combination of both inadequate techology and no market. Then as now, 90 percent of the scientists who had ever lived were alive. There were, however, far fewer of them. There were only perhaps a dozen scientists who could have used the analytical engine or absorbed its output.

There may have been another reason, but it's hard to prove. It involves political ideology. Although Charles Babbage was independently wealthy, as were most educated persons of the day, and although a great deal of his personal fortune was spent on his inventions, his work on the analytical engine was supported by grants from the British government. Babbage wasn't forced to produce to meet a market need, but rather to satisfy his own driving dream.

But Charles Babbage left us a legacy. He described in the language of his time the basic principles of today's electronic computers. A modern computer has:

a. an input facility through which basic information can be entered;
b. a program of basic operating instructions, which is either stored in the machine or inserted by means of the input;
c. a memory in which to store both the information and the instructions, including data that's computed by the machine;
d. a central processing unit (CPU) to process the information according to the program instructions;
e. a means to alert the human operator if more instructions or data is necessary or if something goes wrong;
f. an output device such as a video display screen or printer, which reports the results of the operation to a human being.

That's all there is to *any* computer. It doesn't make any difference if the computer is an Oriental abacus, a slide rule, a pocket calculator, a personal computer, or one of the big mainframe computers—every computer in the world has these components, and they work together as shown in the figure below. The boxes may be very complex inside, but nobody but a computer designer, programmer, or repairman cares about this. The arrows indicate how the information can flow back and forth between these boxes.

The "input" can be a keypad operated by a human being, a

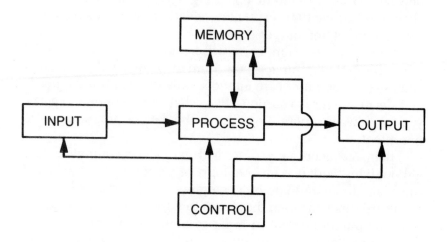

telephone line and "modem" connection, which allows another computer or a remote keypad to provide input, or a tape or disk machine. The purpose of the input device is to give the computer instructions and to provide it with the data or information it will process.

The "memory" is Babbage's "store," in which information, data, and instructions, all in the form of numbers standing for other symbols, is tucked away by the machine in such a way that the machine can find the information again. Data can be put into the memory either by the input or by the processor.

The "processor" is the actual computer. It's the Babbage "mill" where numbers are compared, added, subtracted, multiplied (sequentially added), or divided (sequentially subtracted) according to the logical commands of the program in the form of numbers standing for operations such as "and," "or," "nor," "equal to," "not equal to," etc.

The "output" reports the computer's results. It is instructed to do this by the program. The output device may be a video display terminal, which has a screen upon which the results appear. Or it may be a printer, which types the results on paper. Or it may be a modem device (a contraction of its functional name, "modulator-demodulator"), which connects the computer to a telephone line so that it may transmit the results to a terminal, printer, or other computer on the other end of the telephone line.

All these features are built into the human brain. The brain, however, uses a different operating system, one based upon chemistry rather than crystalline electronics and using vastly different input and output devices.

Someday soon computers will be able to design and build other computers. But for now human beings tell computers what to do. Computers are intended only to serve human needs and desires. And if you don't like what the computer reports, you can always ignore it or change the data or program you've put into it.

Babbage accurately described a modern computer. And although his work was ignored for nearly a century, it may make the basic understanding of a computer easier for people today. Many are shocked when they learn that they don't have to know how computers operate in order to make computers work for them. You don't have to understand the binary numbering system of bits and bytes that a computer uses or the hexadecimal number system with which it crunches these bits and bytes. You don't have to be a programmer to use the programs available. After all, a motorist doesn't have to know the intimate details of the automobile engine that propels the vehicle in order to drive to the grocery store.

Robert Townsend was perhaps the first noncomputer person to cut through to the essence of this principle when he wrote in his book *Up the Organization* in 1970: "First get it through your head that computers are big, expensive, fast, dumb adding-machine-typewriters."

Since 1970, of course, computers have become small, inexpensive, fast, dumb adding-machine-typewriters. Computers are so stupid that they can do only what a human being tells them to do. And they are not complicated. But computers are run by rigid logic, and most people aren't. This is where most of the human-computer problems begin.

3

The Dawn of the Computer Age

Although Charles Babbage laid the conceptual foundation for the modern computer, he was working with only one of three types of machines envisioned by dreamers in the nineteenth century. Work on these three machine types went on almost independently, with no one realizing that they were basically all the same device. The "grand synthesis," or bringing together, of these three lines of development in the twentieth century made possible an entirely new device capable of doing not only everything the three separate types were capable of, but other operations that none of them could do by themselves.

This is a textbook case of a research-and-development (R&D) principle called "serendipity." In legend, the princes of Serendip (now Sri Lanka) went on quests looking for specific treasures, only to stumble on riches far more valuable, which they hadn't known were there when they'd started out.

It is also a case of "synergy," that is, when the sum of the parts, taken together, is more than the individual parts. In the development of the computer, the combination of the three types of machines produced a synergistic result far greater than the mere sum of their individual parts or capabilities.

The three types of machines that underwent parallel development for nearly a century were the *calculating* machine, the *statistical* machine, and the *logical* machine.

It isn't necessary to know the precise technical details of how these machines worked. In the nineteenth century, they were wondrous conglomerations of moving machinery. Today, they are only examples of old, outmoded, obsolete technology. But to understand the computer industry and where it might go, it is indeed helpful to know what these three machine categories actually did, and are still capable of doing, in their modern forms.

The work of Charles Babbage involved the calculating machine. This type of machine was considered necessary for performing the laborious mathematical operations involved in creating tables of numbers and for the equally long and messy computations required for scientific purposes. They also found a role in commerce, where an increasing demand to process more and more numbers became an overwhelming problem. Mechanical adding machines and "arithmometers" had become fairly common by 1900. Although even the mechanical machines were faster than some human beings, they were far slower when they were used for multiplication and division. These two arithmetic activities involve complex procedures, which stretched the capabilities of the slow mechanical calculating machines. Multiplication is basically sequential, repetitive addition, and division is sequential, repetitive subtraction. Therefore, lengthy scientific computations involving many numbers with many integers were done using tables of logarithms.

"Difference engines" of the sort initially developed by Babbage in 1823 continued to be built, due in part to the success of the original Babbage machine (as contrasted to his analytical engine). These devices were used to produce tables for navigation, astronomy, and insurance. Navigators of oceangoing ships depended on precise tables of tides, sunrise, sunset, daily moon position, and position of stars (for celestial navigation). Astronomers needed tables of lunar, planetary, and stellar positions. And insurance companies had an absolutely critical need for actuarial tables derived from morbidity data, lest they go broke writing too many life insurance policies and charging premiums that were too low. Perhaps five such difference engines had been built by 1900.

In contrast to the early mechanical machines of the "digital" sort, which worked with discrete numbers or integers, a number of "analog" machines were also developed. The difference between a digital and an analog machine is the same as that between the old slide rule (an analog device) and an adding machine (a digital device). The slide rule uses *length* as an analog to a number or quantity, whereas an adding machine actually counts discrete gear teeth as indivisible numbers. Sir William Thompson, Lord Kelvin, built an analog tide predictor in 1873. By 1876, his brother James had devised a mechanism for integrating or "adding together" quantities. This was the ball-and-disk integrator. It was subsequently used on many analog machines, including naval gunnery computers, until as recently as 1946. In the nineteenth century, a few analog calculating machines were developed to predict tides in Britain and the United States.

But it was the digital machine that made the greatest progress. By 1890, mechanical calculating machines of several types and makes were in limited use. The "industry" producing these machines was both primitive and rudimentary because the number of machines was limited and so were the available markets. The concept of a useful calculating machine hadn't penetrated deeply into the existing commercial enterprises of the time, although many large companies were burdened with armies of clerks to perform various bookkeeping functions.

As mechanical machine tool technology improved and it became possible to make more accurate parts, and as some elements of the watchmaker's craft began to be incorporated into the infant calculating machine technology, a number of increasingly more complex machines were invented and produced. Some of them, in modern disguise, can still be seen in some commercial activities that haven't yet become totally computerized. But look quickly for them, because mechanical calculating machines, even in their most modern and advanced forms, are rapidly disappearing from the business scene. They may all be in museums before the year 2000.

One of the earliest of these machines was the Thomas arithmometer of about 1850. It operated with a rack-and-pinion mechanical gear assembly. Its carry-over arithmetic function, which put a number into the next higher decimal column, was very much like the gear system that drives the mechanical odometer in an automobile speedometer assembly. However, it had only one place, or "register," in which to store a number. Similar arithmometers were available for home and personal use by the 1930s and had been reduced to pocket size by 1955, shortly before they were rendered obsolete by the electronic pocket calculator.

Another very popular early machine was developed in Russia in 1874 by a Swedish engineer, W. T. Odhner. It utilized the mechanical principle of a pin either pushed into or extracted from a wheel to indicate the presence of a number in the machine. In his factory in St. Petersburg (now Leningrad), Odhner sold more than thirty thousand of his calculators, mostly in Russia, until the revolution, after which his factory was nationalized. Salvaging his documents and blueprints, he moved his operation to Sweden, where, as Original-Odhner, it has continued to the present time, making it one of the oldest computer manufacturing companies in the world.

Another step in the development of the modern computer was the statistical machine. This class of machine was designed to find the relationships between pieces of information and to tabulate large masses of data. In short, it was intended for use with statistics.

In the nineteenth century, the statistical point of view was still very new. Few people understood it. Fewer yet were able to use it to correlate their observations and data and draw general conclusions from this mass of information. But there was a growing need for this kind of technique and for a machine or machines to assist. Even today, scientists and engineers generate what is facetiously referred to as "wall-to-wall data" and then have problems relating it in such a way that valid conclusions can be drawn. If we think that the proliferation of data is great today, can you imagine what it would have been 150 years ago without machines to help? There was an increasing amount of information being accumulated by the sciences, technology, commercial business, and growing governments.

Charles Darwin, a friend of Charles Babbage, was forced to utilize statistics. He had to make sense out of the mass of data he'd collected aboard the *Beagle* and elsewhere. Without statistical analysis, he could not have come to the conclusions about evolution that he published in his book *The Origin of the Species* in 1859. He remarked, probably as much in exasperation as frustration: "My mind seems to have become a kind of machine for grinding general laws out of large collections of facts."

Darwin was so successful in his use of statistical analysis that other scientists, notably Sir Francis Galton (1822-1911), took note and applied the techniques to such studies as meteorology, where there is either too much data or none at all. Lambert Adolphe Jacques Quetelet (1796-1874), a Belgian astronomer, began conducting statistical analyses of the development of the physical and intellectual qualities of human beings and drew upon statistics to develop his theories of the "average person" as a basic type. As recently as a hundred years ago most of the statistical information about large groups of people simply didn't exist. Quetelet's work inspired a general interest in the use of statistics for social reform. Florence Nightingale wanted to test the effectiveness of social legislation and foresaw that statistics would be of inestimable value in handling the huge quantities of data involved. In analyzing the causes of mortality in Britain's Army of the East during the Crimean War, Nightingale invented a system of graphics called "coxcombs" for displaying the relationships between her information. Few people today know that Florence Nightingale was widely known in her time not as the first member of the nursing profession, but as the "passionate statistician."

The need for manipulating large quantities of data—"information processing," as we call it today—was also growing rapidly in business. Armies of clerks were required to process all the data of businesses that were themselves growing very large and serving more and more people. Accounting and other business-data handling hadn't changed appreciably since the times of ancient Egypt, save for the development of mass production of paper. As a result, business firms' records were months or even years behind what was actually taking place.

The increase in business activity was a direct result of population increase, which was in turn a consequence of improvements in medical techniques, the development of immunology, a decrease in the infant mortality rate, and a general increase in life expectancy. It is difficult today for people to realize that two hundred years ago in the fledgling United States of America approximately 50 percent of the population died before reaching the age of five years. As recently as 1900 (data from prior times wasn't statistically correlated and is therefore not totally reliable), the average life expectancy of a male citizen was only 46.3 years. (Today it's 70 years.) As a matter of fact, the developing or "low-tech" nations of the world are still caught in the ancient pattern; life expectancy for males in the Republic of Chad in central Africa is twenty-nine years.

One of the major requirements for statistical machines grew from the constitutional mandate to take a census of the population every ten years to establish congressional representation. As the population grew, the task of assembling and correlating this census data became more difficult. It might still be processed by the old hand methods had not Francis A. Walker, directing the 1880 census, placed significant emphasis on collecting information beyond that mandated by the Constitution. For example, Walker included for the first time a comprehensive census of manufacturers and began to assemble correlations of census data to determine birth and death rates. Suddenly, the government's data-processing and information-handling abilities became critical. Data from this expanded 1880 census were still being tabulated and interpreted in 1887. The population trend itself was clear; the population increase alone would make the 1890 census even more complex, to say nothing of the added counting burden placed upon it. The census, originally just a head count for legislative representation purposes, had become a national inventory of other population characteristics such as immigration status, health, racial composition, literacy, and employment. The need for workable, reliable statistical data-handling and processing machines suddenly became urgent.

The third type of machine along the road to development of the computer is the logical machine. Basically, this sort of machine uses information about its past performance to determine its next action. In short, it can make its own decisions based upon preprogrammed internal logic—i.e., "if A, then B, but if not A, then C." It is also self-regulating. For example, if an input or a machine operation exceeds a predetermined limit A, it will then do B. Otherwise, it will perform operation C. Or do nothing at all.

A simple example of a logical machine is the home thermostat. If the room temperature (A) becomes less than the minimum desired room temperature that's set into the thermostat (B), operation C is begun: the furnace is turned on. When the room temperature (A) exceeds a predetermined maximum temperature (D), operation E is commanded: the furnace is turned off. The thermostat is not only a logical machine, it is also a robot. Today it would also be considered a computer, albeit an extremely crude one. But it is an excellent example of automation that depends upon the principles of programmed machines, feedback, and control theory.

It's also based on a strange form of mathematical notation that enables logical expressions to be written down and logical problems solved. This was first published in 1854 by the English mathematician and logician George Boole (1815-1864) in a work entitled *An Investigation of the Laws of Thought on Which Are Founded the Mathematical Theories of Logic and Probabilities*. Boole's method of logical problem solving is called Boolean algebra. Even a rudimentary knowledge of it is not necessary to understand computers, which operate because of it, or of the development of the computer.

Boole wasn't the first or the last person to develop highly involved and complex mathematical procedures that relate to modern computers. All computers and, in fact, most science and technology, are based on some manner of mathematical foundation. If you're going to do research in certain fields or develop products based on certain technologies, it's necessary to know these mathematical foundations. But not if you're just going to use the gadgetry.

The pure logical machine was initially developed to solve knotty problems in logic. Such problems are not only considered today to be "games," but actually must be solved in various fields of science and in everyday activities in the fields of technology, business, and government. In fact, as the modern computer has matured and become more ubiquitous, people have been using the logical machine aspect of it to solve knotty logic problems dealing with management and administration. But that would hardly have been true—and logic itself would have seemed a pretty useless mental exercise—if logical machines or "automata" hadn't taken over most of the mental work.

One of the first really good logical machines was built in 1883 by Allan Marquand (1853-1924). The son of Henry Gurdon Marquand, a financier and one of the founders and presidents of New York City's Metropolitan Museum of Art, Marquand was a tutor of logic at Princeton University and later a professor of art history. He devised a logical machine far superior to any of the primitive logical machines that had preceded it. A mechanic's nightmare, it was operated by rods and levers, catgut strings, and spiral springs. The Marquand logical machine could handle the following premises from Lewis Carroll's book *Symbolic Logic:*

> No birds, except ostriches, are nine feet high;
> There are no birds in this aviary that belong to anyone but me;
> No ostrich lives on mince pies;
> I have no birds less than 9 feet high.

What is the logical conclusion of this set of premises? No fair running them through your own microcomputer. Marquand's logical machine in 1883 would draw the logical conclusion: "No bird in this aviary lives on mince pies."

Marquand then proceeded to draw up a circuit diagram for operating his machine electrically using relays and switches. This is the first known design of an electrically operated computer.

Marquand carried on extensive correspondence with Charles Sanders Peirce (1839-1914), the son of Benjamin Peirce, a famous Harvard mathematician and astronomer. Although his father expected him to become a scientist, the young Peirce joined the U.S. Coastal Survey in 1861 and remained there for thirty years. He researched and taught in such areas as logic, physics, criminology, classical Greek pronunciation, and philosophy. Later recognized as one of the greatest logicians of all time, he founded the philosophy of pragmatism. It was Peirce who suggested to Marquand in a letter that a logical machine could be created with batteries, switches, and relays. Furthermore, he suggested that such a machine could be hooked up to solve very difficult problems in algebra and geometry. He is the true father of today's electronic computer.

Most logical machines, however, were mechanical, and perhaps the most fascinating one was developed by Annibale Pastore, a professor of philosophy at the University of Genoa in Italy. Pastore's logical machine was mechanically simple: three pulleys and three belts connected them. There were 256 belt combinations, which could represent 256 logical syllogisms. For example, the Pastore machine could handle the truth or falsity of a statement such as:

> Whatever is simple does not dissolve;
> The soul does not dissolve;
> Therefore, the soul is simple.

When the belt connections were made corresponding to both premises and the conclusion, the operator would turn a crank on one pulley. If the syllogism was invalid, as this one is, the pulleys would not budge.

Another logical machine that goes back to 1787 is the flying ball speed governor, actually invented by Sir Isaac Newton, but first put to use by James Watt on his steam engine. The faster a shaft turns, the farther two masses are forced outward by centrifugal force against gravity and the higher on the rotating shaft a control collar is raised. The higher the collar, the more retarded the steam-control throttle. And vice versa. The machine regulates itself.

The history of computers involves history from other apparently unrelated fields of endeavor. As in other areas of scientific and technical history, one must deal with systems rather than with the artificial boundary lines that people establish around technologies and "disciplines." This is nowhere more evident than in the logical machine. Who would have thought that the need to control a loom for weaving complex fabrics would contribute the punched card to the computer industry? Or predate the seminal work of Charles Babbage?

Joseph Marie Jacquard (1752-1834) was a French inventor working in the high-technology industry of the time: textile weaving. In order to weave a complex pattern into a brocade or carpet, the warp or machine-direction yarns must be separated in various sequences to permit the shuttle with the woof yarn to cross the machine. On very large looms weaving fabrics in complex patterns, the loom operator used to be forced to determine and manually set the up or down position of each warp yarn "picker" before each passage of the shuttle. Then in about 1800 in Lyons, France, Jacquard came up with the idea of controlling the up or down position of the warp yarn pickers by means of an automatic linkage controlled by holes punched in wooden cards. If there was a hole in the card, the yarn whose picker was controlled by that card position would be lifted. No hole, no lift. On or off, up or down. Yes or no. Today, we'd call this a binary (two-numbered) logic system. Jacquard cards were connected in a belt so that the pattern could be repeated in the textile at desired intervals.

Even before Jacquard's time some musical instruments had been programmed to perform automatically, controlled by rolls of punched paper. The old player piano is a relic of this type. Nobody knows if Jacquard had seen a player piano and, recalling that device, whose inventor is unknown, "borrowed" the idea for loom control. Or perhaps he saw a similar device, the mechanical music box, said to have been invented in 1776 by Aristed Janvier. (As in any field of human endeavor, the true inventor of a concept or device is often difficult to determine. And with the communication and information explosion, it's going to get even more difficult.)

Some looms are still controlled by Jacquard cards today. (Once something becomes established as workable, it tends to be retained even when better things come along. "If it works, don't fix it." This is especially true in old, established low-technology endeavors. We will see this happen in the high-tech world of computers, too.)

One cannot discuss logical machines without mentioning the chess-playing automata, the ultimate in logical devices. The most notorious one was built in the late eighteenth century by the Austrian inventor and mechanic Wolfgang von Kempelen (1734-1804). It allegedly had a mechanical man to move the chess players and featured a machinelike voice. In actuality, the machine had a small man cleverly hidden inside it. It was, however, the forerunner of all of today's chess-playing computers and, even though it was a fraud, stimulated and continues to stimulate people to perfect chess-playing automata. The modern chess automata are, of course, electronic and controlled by microelectronic chips; some of them, like the von Kempelen machine, also have machine voices.

By 1890, the basic elements of the computer were in place. Some early mechanical devices had been built. Many of them were at work computing mathematical and astronomical tables. In later decades, however, many computer developers would neglect the nineteenth-century developments and would, in essence, reinvent the wheel. But what was most important to the dawning computer industry was the simple fact that the one critical factor in every industry was beginning to take shape: the market.

There was a perceived need for the computer in several fields of endeavor. And there was a primitive technology that could begin to respond to that market.

4

The First Computer Companies

In the field of information processing, the dam broke between 1886 and 1890. There were then over sixty million people in the United States who had to be counted in the regular census of 1890. It was estimated by the Census Office that the hand tabulation of this data into categories of sex, birthplace, and occupation alone would require the efforts of a hundred clerks for a period of seven years and eleven months. Quite obviously, the census data would have been obsolete once it had undergone even this rudimentary tabulation. There were two options: go to a fast, accurate form of mechanical tabulation or narrow the scope of the 1890 census. The latter option was unthinkable. The results of the 1880 census were proving to be extremely valuable not only to the federal government, but also to commercial businesses.

So the Census Office held a competition to select an efficient system for census tabulation. There were three entries. William C. Hunt proposed a system using colored cards. It required hand sorting and counting. It wasn't much of an improvement over existing systems of hand tabulation. Charles F. Pidgin's system used color-coded paper "chips." Like Hunt's system, it also required hand sorting and counting. The easy winner was a system using punch cards and electrical counting, which promised to do the job in less than half the time of the two competing systems. It was proposed by a young mining engineer and statistician named Herman Hollerith.

Born in 1860, Hollerith graduated from Columbia University School of Mines at age nineteen. For four years he worked in the U.S. Census Office. Then he spent a short time as a clerk in the Patent Office, after which he set himself up as an independent engineer. His work at the Census Office and the Patent Office had put him in contact with many government officials. (One must remember that the federal government in those days was a fraction of the size it is today. Thus, nearly every civil service employee knew personally or by reputation nearly every other civil servant in the town of Washington, D.C.) Hollerith had made the acquaintance of the U.S. medical librarian, J. S. Billings, who encouraged him to think about a method of tabulating important vital medical data such as birth and mortality statistics. A population of around sixty million people was beginning to pose problems in the collection and correlation of this data, which had become an important part of public health planning.

Hollerith got the idea of using perforated rolls of paper tape. One suspects that he must have been familiar with the player piano, which was a standard feature of the home parlor of the period. A player piano uses a roll of perforated paper tape to store the information necessary to get the piano mechanism to play. Hollerith probably borrowed the concept.

But one day while riding a train, he noticed the railroad conductor punching tickets. The punched railway ticket stores data reliably and permanently. It is a smaller module than a roll of paper tape and is more easily handled. A great deal of information about a specific item can be punched into it.

This inspired Herman Hollerith to reinvent the wheel. He took the principle of the punched railway ticket and the punch card used to control a Jacquard loom and applied it to data processing. It is doubtful if, in his education as a mining engineer, he'd seen a Jacquard loom. But he may have heard of it or read about it; he was, after all, an educated young man. And, of course, Charles Babbage had proposed the use of Jacquard-like punch cards to run the unfinished analytical engine fifty years earlier.

Hollerith developed an information-processing and handling system with these borrowed ideas. Data was manually punched into cards using Hollerith's pantographic punch. When the card puncher placed the pointer in one of the coded holes on the face of the punch, a corresponding hole was punched through a blank card that had been inserted into the back of the punch. The original Hollerith card was a matrix of round holes, 16 across by 12 vertically, allowing a possibility of 192 holes to appear in the card. It was a binary, or two-numbered (zero and one), system; either the hole was in the card or not. Today we would call it a 192-bit memory system. The information collected for each person was punched into a card, and each possible answer was assigned a specific location of a hole or holes in the card.

Hollerith's card reader was also simple, but it was the first data-processing system that used electricity. The card with the data punched into it was mechanically positioned on a flat plate. A vertically movable plate was then pressed down on the card. The movable plate contained 192 pins, one for every possible hole in the card, and the pins were connected to an electrical source. Where there was a hole in the card, the pin passed through into a mercury-filled cup below, thereby completing an electrical circuit. Each completed electrical circuit caused an electromagnet to advance a counting dial by one number. There were forty such dials on a Hollerith "tabulator," allowing answers to forty questions to be counted simultaneously.

The system could also sort cards in a semiautomatic manner. The lids on the compartments of the sorting box would open in response to specific holes or combinations of holes. After running the card through the reader and having the sorter open the lid on a box, the human operator then dropped the card into that box and closed the lid by hand.

Hollerith was granted U.S. Patent Number 395,781 for his system.

It sounds primitive today, but in 1886, when Hollerith first used his system to compile mortality statistics for the city of Baltimore, it was a quantum jump in the ability to process, sort, and store data. The U.S. Surgeon General's Office used it for similar purposes in 1889. When the Census Office competition came along, Hollerith could not only propose a new concept for tabulating the census data, but could also point to a successful track record. He didn't just have an invention, he had a system that worked.

This was the start of the computer revolution. Even in 1890, it was revolutionary.

It was also the start of the first company in the computer industry, Hollerith's Electric Tabulating Company, whose subsequent history can be traced through mergers, acquisitions, and takeovers to today's computer firms. But that's getting ahead of our story.

For the 1890 census, 46,804 census takers completed forms for each family or household in the United States. There were about thirteen million of them, representing a total population of 62,979,766. The census book tabulating population location was available one year and seven months after the start of tabulation. Hand tabulation, as previously pointed out, would have taken an estimated seven years and eleven months to produce the same results, and probably with a larger percentage of error.

Scientific American, then a weekly magazine of "practical information, art, science, mechanics, chemistry, and manufactures," showed the Hollerith equipment on the cover of its issue of August 20, 1890. The *Electrical Engineer*, a professional journal, devoted its November 1891 issue to the subject "Counting a Nation by Electricity" and remarked: "This apparatus works unerringly as the mills of the gods, but beats them all hollow as to speed."

But there were reliability problems. As one might suspect, the machines suffered from occasional mechanical failures. But these happened for different reasons than one might suspect, even given the rudimentary electrical and mechanical technology of 1890. As one of the contemporary Census Office machine operators candidly reported: "The trouble was usually that somebody had extracted the mercury from one of the little cups with an eyedropper and squirted it into a spittoon, just to get an un-needed rest."

Herman Hollerith viewed the results somewhat dispassionately: "I will have in future years the satisfaction of being the first statistical engineer." He would also have the satisfaction of becoming the first computer millionaire.

Buoyed by his achievement and with a highly successful

series of applications behind him, Hollerith went international. The success of the 1890 U.S. Census didn't go unnoticed in the rest of the world. Canada purchased Hollerith machines for their own census. Austria used Hollerith machines built in Austria by Otto Schaffler. High technology in the computer industry was then exported without fear or rancor. In fact, in 1895, Herman Hollerith went to Moscow for the specific purpose of selling his machines to the Russians.

The Russians had never taken a general census because the problems of transportation and communication in the Eurasian heartland made it very difficult to get to everyone. But Hollerith was determined to sell his tabulating equipment to the czar. His principal effort was aimed at starting up a census. After months of negotiations Hollerith finally got a contract with the czar, and the Russians got the equipment necessary to tabulate the results of their very first census, taken in 1897. The next census didn't occur until 1927, probably using the same thirty-year-old Hollerith machines.

Herman Hollerith went on to develop faster and more versatile versions of his original punch-card machines. Miniaturization of mechanical parts and assemblies was made possible by continual progress in machine tools, as well as an integration of the watchmaker's craft into the technology. It became possible to punch many more holes in a card and read the holes either mechanically or electrically. Hollerith redesigned his punch-card format and increased its size.

He also made the Hollerith card larger to enable more data to be punched into it. In doing so, he standardized the size of the Hollerith card (erroneously called the "IBM card" in some places) on a worldwide basis for many years to come. Even his competitors had to build their machines to handle the Hollerith card because it was so ubiquitous. Like many worldwide standards, it was established in a surprisingly accidental, illogical, and arbitrary manner. Herman Hollerith chose to make the improved punch card the same size as the dollar bill of the time. The size of the dollar bill has grown smaller since, but the Hollerith card has remained the same over the years.

Hollerith was a creative inventor, an engineer, and a salesman. He was not a manager, and he made business mistakes with his Electric Tabulating Company. The first of these was renting his tabulating machines to the U.S. Census Office instead of selling them outright, as he had done in Russia. This didn't lock the bureaucracy into using his system until they'd worn out the machines or they had become obsolete. As a result, in 1905 the Census Office decided to stop leasing tabulating machines from Hollerith and build their own.

The second mistake Hollerith made was not holding on to his people. He created his own competition. His trusted assistant, the Russian-born James Powers, left and went to work for the Census Office. There, Powers invented a new electrical card punch, which was used in the 1910 census and won a grand prize at the 1915 Pan-Pacific Exposition in San Francisco. In 1911, Powers resigned and went to work for Philo Remington.

This was the Remington of the famed firearms firm. Having made a mess of developing the typewriter of C. L. Scholes (after spending thirteen years creating the market for the typewriter as an office machine, he bailed out just as the market was beginning to develop), Remington saw another way to utilize the mechanical expertise of his firearms company in building the new tabulating machines. Powers developed new card-sorting machines, one of which sensed cards mechanically instead of electrically. He also worked out a new printing tabulator.

Meanwhile, another company was getting itself into the data-processing business, but by a far different route.

As specialized industries develop and evolve, areas of technology that once seemed to have no relationship whatsoever to the primary technology become integrated into it. The development of the cash register is one such example.

A cash register is now recognized as a device that records retail sales and, as such, is an integral part of commercial data processing. But it didn't start out that way. And it didn't appear to have anything in common with Hollerith's punch-card statistical machines.

A Dayton, Ohio, restaurant owner, James Ritty, came up with the idea of the cash register in the engine room of an oceanliner. On a trip to Europe in the summer of 1878, Ritty saw an instrument that counted the revolutions of the ship's propeller shaft. He decided that if a device could mechanically measure and record what was going on in the engine room of a ship, a machine could be developed to measure and make records of the business transactions in his restaurants. (One of the big problems in those days was to prevent the hired help from pocketing cash without recording the transaction.)

James Ritty had a brother, John, who was a mechanic and inventor. Together, the Ritty brothers completed the first cash register in 1879. It had two rows of keys across the front and a large clocklike dial that, controlled by the keys, displayed the dollars and cents of the sale. It didn't have a cash drawer, only two locked-in disks that accumulated rung-up sales made during the course of the day. Their second model had some improvements, and they got a patent on the cash register on November 4, 1879. Their third model, called "Ritty's Incorruptible Cashier," featured a pop-up tablet indicating the amount of the rung-up transaction; this feature is retained by cash registers even today, but has become an electronic display. Further development resulted in the first machine offered for sale to merchants and featured a roll of paper that was perforated to record sales; at the end of the day, the proprietor or his clerk would remove the roll of paper, count holes, and have a record of each sale plus a sales total.

Ritty managed to sell only *one* cash register. It was purchased by John H. Patterson for use in his retail coal business in Coalton, Ohio.

So in October 1881, James Ritty sold his cash register business, along with all the patent rights, to Jacob H. Eckert of Cincinnati for $1,000.

Eckert was a salesman. He thought he could sell cash registers or anything else. He did reasonably well at it. Less than a year after he bought out Ritty, he was selling enough to realize he couldn't handle it alone. With four other men, he organized the National Manufacturing Company with a capital stock of $10,000 (later increased to $15,000) and retained controlling interest. To the cash register Eckert added the locking cash drawer and the "bell heard round the world," which added the term "ringing up a sale" to our vocabulary.

John H. Patterson, Ritty's one and only customer, was so impressed with the savings that his cash register produced that he bought twenty-five shares of stock in the National Manufacturing Company and became both its secretary and a director. Eckert, however, wasn't doing so well with cash register sales because of both proprietor skepticism and employee resistance to the product. When Patterson sold his coal business and retired from his position as director and secretary of Eckert's firm, the company was operating at such a loss that he could sell only five of his twenty-five shares. During a trip west, Patterson met a New England merchant on vacation in Colorado Springs and asked why the man was able to take such an extended vacation. The vacationing merchant told him: "I have a capable manager and a cash register made in Dayton." The incident served to restimulate John Patterson's interest. With his brother, Frank, he returned to Dayton and purchased control of the National Manufacturing Company. He met with such ridicule even from the officers of the company that he got angry. "I am going into the cash register business and make a success of it," he vowed.

The first Dayton factory was only thirty-two hundred square feet, and the payroll included thirteen employees. Production was four cash registers per week. But because of Patterson's determination, by 1888 the company moved into the first factory specifically designed to manufacture data-processing machines—cash registers. It was a multilevel building with sixteen thousand square feet of space.

Shortly after buying the company, John H. Patterson changed its name. It became the National Cash Register Company.

For the next forty years, the company manufactured and marketed cash registers. It took that long for the device to breed other business data machines.

With Hollerith's Electric Tabulating Company and Patterson's National Cash Register Company, the computer industry had its first two fledgling firms and was off the ground at the beginning of the twentieth century.

5

The Business of Business Machines

Business in the past was like business today, primarily concerned with keeping track of and counting things, especially money. Data management and information processing has *always* been a necessity in the business world and it has required specialized people. From the days of the ancient civilizations of Sumer and Egypt five thousand years ago until only recently, people variously called scribes, clerks, and bookkeepers did this tedious work.

As the centuries went by, various unknown geniuses developed devices to assist people in this work. No one knows when and where the Oriental abacus, the first digital computer, was invented. Today it is still found all over the world and has one important advantage over the pocket calculator: it doesn't need an electrical power supply such as a battery, an important factor in many developing countries where such modern marvels as lithium button cells aren't readily available.

The lot of a bookkeeper or clerk in 1884 seems incredible now. For eight to twelve hours a day, six to seven days a week, he'd spend all his time seated on a hard stool or chair hunched over a desk covered with papers on which were columns and columns of numbers.

There were no women clerks. If they were hired at all, they

had to take production-line work such as sewing and machine tending. Being a bookkeeper or clerk required an extraordinary mental capacity for sustained concentration, extreme attention to detail, and a passion for accuracy. In large banks and businesses with their great volumes of numbers, the task of the bookkeeper and clerk was also physically formidable and strenuous. At the time it was believed that only men were suited for this sort of work.

As the pressures of business growth increased following the Civil War, some companies began hiring men trained as rapid calculators. Then as now, there was a profusion of "how-to" books on the subject. W. K. David, the "practical rapid accountant," promised the readers of his book *The New Practical Lightning Calculator* that "those who diligently examine this book's contents will learn to reckon with phenomenal accuracy and rapidity, and reach a sphere above the ordinary accountant."

"Lightning calculators" were popular stage entertainers in the 1880s. Men who could add a column of ten four-digit numbers instantly were not unusual on the vaudeville circuit. Scientists, as well as theatergoers, were intrigued with this mental phenomenon. It was the general belief in those days, especially in Europe, that science should strive to understand everything possible. (In the United States the need for a practical application of technology pushed aside, as it often does today, the basic research of science.) In France, the Academie des Sciences appointed a committee to study the mental processes of the lightning calculators of the stage; the practical lightning bookkeepers of industry were far too busy making a living to be bothered with such scientific nonsense.

The business pressures on these unusual men took its toll though, to say nothing of the mental and physical debilitation of ordinary bookkeepers. A news item of the late 1800s from Belgrade, then the capital of Serbia, is indicative of the problem: "Damian Stanislitz, station master of Yogondin, was so upset at finding a deficit of $1.25 in his accounts that he committed suicide after writing the railway company stating his error. When his accounts were examined, it was proved that an error in casting up [carrying forward] had led him astray. There was not a penny missing."

The sustained work of adding long columns of figures was

"turning men into veritable machines," according to Dorr E. Felt.

"Calculating power alone should seem to be the least human of qualities," wrote Oliver Wendell Holmes.

And the president of Harvard, Charles Eliot, said: "A man ought not to be employed at a task which a machine could perform."

Various men tried various approaches to alleviating this problem.

In 1892 at the age of twenty-eight, John K. Gore left his teaching position in mathematics at the Woodbridge School in New York to join the Prudential Insurance Company as an actuary. Prudential had an extensive statistical department to handle its actuarial data. Although Gore rose to become vice-president of the firm in 1912, his early years with the company as an actuary convinced him that the firm needed a mechanical way of handling data. He noted that people were being worn out by long hours of tedious calculations, were thus prone to make more mistakes, which in turn produced errors in the actuarial data and cost the company money.

It's quite probable that Gore had read of or heard about the Hollerith tabulating machines used in the 1890 census. Gore drew up rough sketches of a card-perforating machine and card sorter of his own design. His brother-in-law, a mechanical engineer, helped him build them. Gore invented the multiple-key punch, which also automatically ejected the punched card as a new card was brought into position; this speeded up the process of key-punching the data. Gore's sorter was driven by an electric motor and was arranged in four tiers of circular bins, each containing ten card compartments. For ordering cards before inserting them into machines, Gore taught Prudential clerks to count cards by listening to the sound they made as they were riffled under the thumb.

Gore's key-punch and card-sorting machines were installed in 1895. Prudential used them well into the 1930s.

But the business-machine market really got under way in the 1890s with two machines, designed and built independently, that did the same sort of arithmetic work. They became the most popular accounting machines in the world and are still used today in offices that haven't become computerized.

Dorr E. Felt, quoted earlier, was a Chicago accountant and

inventor. He knew the incredible pressures on a bookkeeper and decided to build a mechanical adding machine. He wanted his machine to outperform accountants and clerks. "I knew that many accountants could mentally add four columns of figures at a time," he remarked, "so I decided that I must beat that in designing my machines." He describes how he set about this task:

> It was near Thanksgiving Day of 1884, and I decided to use the holiday in construction of the wooden model. I went to the grocers and selected a box which seemed to me about the right size for the casing. It was a macaroni box, so I have always called it the macaroni box model. For keys, I procured some meat skewers from the butcher around the corner and some staples from a hardware store for the key guides and an assortment of elastic bands to be used for springs. When Thanksgiving Day came I got up early and went to work with a few tools, principally a jack knife.

In 1886, Felt got his employer, Robert Tarrant, to sponsor his invention; within a year, Felt was a full partner in Tarrant's company. The adding machine they produced was known as the Comptometer.

The Comptometer's use spread beyond the accounting profession. Save for an analog computer called the slide rule (invented in 1614 by the Scottish mathematician John Napier), the Comptometer was the first digital calculating machine used in engineering work. By 1895, the United States Navy was using Comptometers for almost all the engineering calculations required for warship construction.

Another accountant who knew the problems of the profession well was William Seward Burroughs (1857-1898). Born in Rochester, New York, the son of a mechanic, Burroughs was a slight, retiring man who was always in precarious health. He went to work in the counting room of a bank in Auburn, New York. By the time he was twenty-four years old, the long hours required to sum columns of figures, the interminable search for the inevitable mistakes, and the tedious drudgery of a clerk's job took its toll on his already poor health. He was advised by his doctors to go to a warmer climate and change his occupation.

He chose to move to St. Louis, Missouri, and to take up the trade of his father. As a mechanic, he determined to design and build a machine that would add long columns of numbers mechanically.

In 1882, Burroughs was in St. Louis working for a machine shop owner, Joseph Boyer, who gave him bench space to develop his machine. Unlike Felt, Burroughs didn't write down the details of his development. It fell to his employer to recall what took place over the next two years:

> There was Burroughs with his great idea, greater than any of us could fully appreciate, and with his meager capital of $300. Long before the first model was actually begun, his money was gone. But as his resources dwindled, his courage rose. I used to leave him at his bench in the evening and find him still there in the morning. . . . When damp weather expanded the paper on which he worked, he resorted to polished sheets of copper, cutting his lines with the point of a needle. When he located the center, he did so under the microscope. When the polished copper proved tiresome to his eyes, he drew on polished zinc, chemically blackened, the lines showing white against the background of black. It was his way of drafting plans for what he knew must be minutely accurate.

In 1885, at the age of twenty-eight, Burroughs filed for his first patent. On August 21, 1888, he was granted Patent Number 388,116 for a "Calculating Machine." It was the first patent for an adding and listing machine.

To produce and market his machine, Burroughs got together with Thomas Metcalfe, R. M. Scruggs, and William R. Pye to form the American Arithmometer Company in St. Louis. Metcalfe was elected the first president, Burroughs was named vice-president, William Metcalfe (not a stockholder) was secretary, and Scruggs treasurer. The company's product was a single model, a straight adding and listing machine that printed each entry and the result on a roll of paper tape. It sold for $475.

By 1889, Burroughs had manufactured fifty machines. But they proved almost impossible for anyone but Burroughs himself to operate smoothly and accurately.

There was one exception to this. Burroughs had a field agent who could operate his demonstrator model so well that he refused to sell it. The salesman was making far more money hauling his machine in a wheelbarrow from saloon to saloon, betting drinks and money on its accuracy.

The machines were recalled. Burroughs invented an automatic corrective device that was designed into all subsequent models. The problem was solved. But Burroughs and his salesman had a bad image to overcome. This they did, often by clever means. Some of the new machines, especially the sales demonstrators, were manufactured with glass cases. The visibility of the mechanical inner workings was used as a selling point.

There are no examples of the very first Burroughs adding machine in existence. Shortly after the improved models began to sell well, Burroughs went to the room where the original fifty models were stored and, one by one, hurled them out an open window to the pavement below.

Once the initial problems of accuracy and ease of operation were solved, the Burroughs adding machine grew increasingly popular. The company began to expand. By 1898, ten years after its founding, the company had its own factory and an office staff of sixty-five people, along with assets of more than $300,000. It went international in 1895, establishing the Burroughs Adding and Registering Company, Limited, in Nottingham, England. By 1897, four models were being offered. The original model was a nine-column machine; the second model could make a duplicate copy of the register tape; the third had a wider carriage; and the fourth had only six columns and, as the bottom-of-the-line model, sold for a mere $250. Even at this early date, the trend of price reduction with increased production and improved technology was beginning to make its mark in the fledgling computer industry.

In 1898, the American Arithmometer Company sold 729 machines. William S. Burroughs predicted that the entire U.S. market might absorb as many of 7,800 machines. But in 1905 alone, 7,800 machines were sold. In 1907, the fifty thousandth machine was made.

William S. Burroughs didn't live to see it. He retired from the company because of ill health and died on September 4, 1898. His original St. Louis employer, Joseph E. Boyer, became president of the American Arithmometer Company in 1902.

By 1904, it became obvious that the company had outgrown its St. Louis factory and offices, so it moved to Detroit. On Saturday, October 8, 1904, two special trains pulled out of St. Louis. Their cargo was the entire American Arithmometer Company—foreman and factory hands, wives and children, ice boxes, gramophones, punch presses, rolltop desks, crockery, and adding machines. The destination was a newly constructed plant north of Detroit on land that had been the seed bed for the famous Ferry Seed Company. After the long weekend trip, the 465 employees came to work on Monday morning, unloaded the train, and began operations at the new factory. By the end of the month, 71 machines had been produced. This rose to 316 in December.

In 1905, with assets valued at more than $5 million, the American Arithmometer Company was renamed the Burroughs Adding Machine Company in honor of the man whose vision had led to the founding of the company less than two decades before. In 1953, it became the Burroughs Corporation.

While Burroughs was busily at work satisfying one market need in the business world, back in the Washington, D.C. headquarters of the Electric Tabulating Company Herman Hollerith was kept busy expanding the firm to keep up with the increasing demand for equipment to handle data processing and statistical analysis of large amounts of data. Neither organization yet saw that a synthesis of what they were each doing would someday result in products of a totally new sort to satisfy markets they couldn't dream of.

Large industries such as railroads, insurance companies, and public utilities began applying the Electric Tabulating Company machines to the solutions of their own data-processing problems. As each company extended the use of the punch card to its own accounting system, Hollerith came up with the forty-column card the size of a dollar bill. Cards could be ordered with special layouts and in special colors. The holes were still circular, however. It wasn't until 1924, when the Hollerith card format was changed to eighty columns, that the rectangular hole became standard.

Hollerith probably saw the Burroughs Arithmometer and the Felt Comptometer. Those machines were as ubiquitous in

1905 businesses as the desktop computer is today. Hollerith proceeded to develop an electric adding mechanism, an "electric integrator," and incorporated it into his tabulating equipment so the machinery could add as well as count. The punch-card format itself was redesigned with columns of numbers, essentially the form used today. He also developed a single ten-key punch for all applications.

This advance made it feasible for railroads to use punch-card machines for their waybill statistics—what was shipped, who shipped it, who received it, how much it weighed, what routing was used, how long it took en route, and what the shipping charges were. Before the Hollerith punch-card machines were used, all of this had to be processed by hand. It often took months to get meaningful information to management. And as for tracing a lost shipment, that might never be accomplished. To allow his automatic sorting machines to be installed in the limited space of most railroad freight offices, Hollerith redesigned his sorter and came up with a sturdier vertical machine.

Insurance companies saw what John E. Gore had done at the Prudential Insurance Company. They saw how quickly machine tabulation could correlate actuarial statistics and allow mortality predictions to be made. Public utility companies faced the problem of keeping track of a very large number of very small accounts. They embraced the tabulating machines quickly. Telephone companies also had a large number of transactions to be recorded and billed. (Because of their use of women as telephone switchboard operators, which proved the ability of women to work with complex switchboards, they pioneered the use of women in the bookkeeping end of the business. The typewriter had started the trend of women in business, but the early computer in the form of the tabulating machine reinforced it.)

Hollerith and his engineers saw technology used in another area and were quick to incorporate it into their own designs. From the telephone technology of the time, they appropriated the flexible plugboard. By rearranging the plugs, the information from any column of a punch card could be fed into any register in the sorting and integrating machines. This made it possible to do many different jobs of many different types on one machine without tedious, time-consuming, and error-prone re-wiring. Plugboards are still used in some large main-frame computers today.

As might be expected, there was considerable technical fallout and spinoff as the features of the tabulating and adding machines began to be appreciated in other industries. The machines were first used to replace hand methods in statistical data processing (the census) and accounting. Soon other bright people saw that they could be applied to tasks *that could not have been performed by hand at all*. They could be used to make an *immediate* analysis of costs and sales.

This breakthrough offered a company, any company that picked it up and used it, enormous marketing advantages. Suddenly, after 1910, a great variety of companies began using the new machines—steel mills, department stores, shoe factories, machine shops, meat packers, electric utilities, and government agencies.

Before these early tabulating machines and adding machines became recognized as *business machines*, cost accounting was mostly a matter of sheer guesswork. Nobody knew how much anything really cost to buy, make, store, transport, or sell. It was a matter of "cash in versus cash out." Businesses of all sorts were largely at the mercy of their cash-flow situation. The entire modern concept of credit of all sorts was generally ignored because there was no way to handle it. The larger and more complex the operations of a company became, the more important it was to have an accurate analysis of what was going on.

Using Electric Tabulating, Burroughs, Comptometer, and National Cash Register machines as business machines, a company could set up and operate procedures to find out just how much its products actually cost to make, how well they were selling, where they were selling and where they weren't, what types of customers were buying them, how good their quality control was, and a host of other marketing activities. A larger assortment of products with small differences could be successfully produced and sold at a profit because it was possible to get a handle on subtle product variations that affected costs and pricing.

The business machines began to be used for analysis of

payrolls, purchasing records, inventories, overhead allocations, and shipping costs. Managers could get information they never had before, data that enabled them to make better decisions based on facts rather than conjecture and guesswork. Sales analyses could be made on a daily, weekly, and monthly basis. Sales could be broken down by product line, territory, season, and any other classification management found useful.

The modern theories of time-and-motion and the proper use of manpower could be put to use with the data available from business machines. Frederick W. Taylor's studies of work systems, which he called "scientific management" or "Taylorization," could be implemented. It was the foundation for what later came to be called "the human use of human beings" by another computer pioneer. For example, today men still shovel material into steel furnaces, although much of this has been taken over by automatic feed systems. In 1907, Taylor was hired by the Bethlehem Steel Company to improve factory operations. A typical Taylor finding was "the scientific fact that a first-class shoveler will do his largest day's work when he has a shovel load of 21½ pounds. As a matter of common sense, it was necessary to furnish each workman each day with a shovel that would hold just 21½ pounds of the particular material which he was called upon to shovel."

Other machines were being invented, put into production, and used in business. It wasn't recognized for decades, in some cases, that these were also business machines.

The first computing scale was patented in 1885 by Julius E. Pitrat of Gallipolis, Ohio. His patents resulted in the formation of the Computing Scale Company in Dayton, Ohio, in 1891.

A mechanical time recorder was invented in 1883 by Willard Bundy of Auburn, New York. With his brother Harlow, he organized the Bundy Manufacturing Company to produce them. The company later became the International Time Recording Company.

The first man to see these machines as business machines was banker Charles R. Flint. He arranged the merger of Hollerith's Electric Tabulating Company with the Computing Scale Company and the International Time Recording Company. The new conglomerate was called the Computing-Tabulating-Recording (C-T-R) Company. It came under single management in 1914, when it had thirteen hundred employees. Thomas J. Watson left the National Cash Register Company to become C-T-R's general manager. He soon became president. In 1924, the C-T-R Company adopted the name International Business Machines Corporation.

The computer revolution had begun.

6

Dawn Over
Silicon Valley

In 1905, every mathematical machine—Hollerith's tabulating and sorting machines, Burroughs's adding machines, Felt's Comptometers, and NCR's cash registers—was basically mechanical. Most of them were crank operated, but some were powered by electric motors. The hand crank had already started to go the way of the buggy whip. But because all these miraculous new machines depended on mechanical linkages, cams, gears, and other gadgetry, they suffered from all of the various shortcomings and maladies of every mechanical machine, even those built today.

Mechanical movements produce friction, a force created by the rubbing together of two objects. In some machines, friction was an enemy that had to be reduced by lubrication. In others, friction itself was an operating feature that the mechanism made use of—in belts, press fits, and other applications whose operation depends on the force of friction.

Friction and even the movement of mechanical parts in contact with one another produces wear. This in turn can destroy microscopic dimensional tolerances and turn a precision machine into a pile of worthless junk.

Mechanical devices depend upon the movement of masses in the "works," even though these masses may be extremely small, as in the case of a mechanical, spring-wound wristwatch.

When a physical mass is moved, stopped, or its movement altered in any way, inertia becomes a factor. Inertia is the resistance of any mass to a change in its motion. Inertia resists change. As a result of inertia, change of motion takes time to complete. This means that mechanical devices cannot be made to operate any faster than the inertia of their largest part will permit. As a result, mechanical calculating machines are slow compared to today's standards. This slowness eventually led to their replacement by faster devices.

No mechanical part can be manufactured with zero dimensional tolerances, especially in mass production, where the variance in dimensions follows the statistical rules that hold true in the rest of the universe. There will always be the case where the mass-produced nut won't fit on the mass-produced machine screw because the nut is on the small end of the tolerance gap and the machine screw is on the large end. Although hand-made parts can come closer to absolute zero tolerances, they take longer to make and therefore are much more expensive. They are only considered for a limited number of highly specialized devices. As a result, all mechanical computers have slack, slop, or tolerance in their mechanical parts. This, in turn, can reduce their accuracy or cause them to fail.

All of these factors, and some other minor ones, point to the fact that mechanical computers are large and heavy, they wear out, require maintenance, and are slow. Because the miracle calculating machines were doing such an outstanding job in terms of 1905 demands, few users required greater speeds, smaller sizes, or less maintenance. The shortcomings of the mechanical calculating machines were accepted because their benefits far outweighed these shortcomings. In the course of their continual development and improvement, resulting from both better technology and increased marketplace demands, the machines would someday reach their limits in terms of size, number-handling capabilities, and speed. This didn't occur until about 1940, and mechanical adding machines were still very much in use in many businesses in 1975. (And why not? If a mechanical machine based on old technology is doing the job, why trade it in for a new-technology machine, despite its greater capabilities?)

The solution to the problems inherent in using mechanical

parts whose absolute smallest component is the molecule seems obvious to us today. It wasn't obvious in 1905. Neither was the invention that became the solution obvious.

If mechanical parts based on molecules are too large, then it is necessary to go to operating parts that are smaller: sub-atomic particles. In short, electrons.

But nobody knew how to do this in 1905.

And when someone came up with a way, it was another case of being born too soon.

The vacuum tube has been hailed as one of the greatest inventions of all time and has been compared to the lever and the wheel in terms of its impact upon humanity. The steam engine and the coke oven ushered in the first industrial revolution, replacing human and animal muscle power in the process. Science writer Mitchell Wilson, in his 1954 book *American Science and Invention,* said that what he called the "second industrial revolution"—the replacement of the human nervous system by automatic control devices—had been ushered in by the invention of the vacuum tube.

"Vacuum tube" is the American term for the device. The British call it an "electronic valve." Between 1920 and 1950 electronic engineers called it a "triode." Its inventor, Dr. Lee De Forest, called it an "audion." All of these names do not really describe what it is, what it did, and what it continues to do, even in this era of solid-state electronics.

It was a breakthrough, although it could have been in-vented by several people at an earlier time because all of the physics and background data were known for years. Even at that, De Forest stumbled upon it. The way in which he came upon his great invention is so typical of how technological progress is made that it deserves more than just passing men-tion. In addition to making the modern computer possible, it was one of the first technological innovations made in an area of California known then as the Santa Clara Valley and today as Silicon Valley.

Lee De Forest was born on August 26, 1873, in Council Bluffs, Iowa, the son of the minister of the First Congregational Church. As a boy, he was as much a part of the technology of the time as the whiz-kid computer hackers of today. After his family moved to Talledega, Alabama, and he got to see a blast furnace in nearby Birmingham, he built a model out of an old ash can and used one of the family's heirlooms, an old-fashioned bellows, as his compressed air supply. He became fascinated by locomotives and built a nonoperative one of his own out of packing cases, sugar barrels, kegs, and a tin can for a whistle. When he wasn't playing ball, swimming in the creek with the other boys, learning to play the coronet, and trying to win his fortune in a hundred different ways advertised in *Youth's Companion* magazine, he was sketching the details of pistons and valves for the great engines of his dreams. He always wanted to be an inventor.

For two generations, there had been a special scholarship at Yale for members of the De Forest family. Lee De Forest took advantage of it to attend Yale's Sheffield Scientific School, from which he graduated in 1896. He went on to graduate work under the legendary Yale engineering professor J. Willard Gibbs. His doctoral thesis reflected his continuing development and interest in technological progress; he investigated the recently discovered Hertzian waves, the first breakthrough in what was then called "wireless transmission." After receiving his doctorate in 1899, he went to work for the Western Electric Company in Chicago. But his independence of mind and a love affair diverted him from the routine problems of telephone engineering. One day, his supervisor called him aside and told him bluntly: "De Forest, you'll never make a telephone engineer. As far as I'm concerned, you can go to hell in your own way. Do as you damn please!"

So Lee De Forest did. He devoted all his time and effort to the problems of wireless telegraphy, forming the De Forest Wireless Telegraph Company in 1902 with stock promoter Abraham White, who was authorized to raise $3 million in equity capital by the sale of common stock. De Forest got busy and landed a War Department contract for Signal Corps wireless sets, a Navy contract, and a contract for a wireless radio station chain between Costa Rica and Panama for the United Fruit Company. But Abraham White undercut De Forest by issuing fancy prospectuses and erecting ninety wireless stations across America. Most of these stations never sent a message. In 1907, De Forest discovered that White and other directors were looting the company by selling its assets to a dummy corporation. Lee De Forest resigned, taking with him only those patents that were pending, including the most important one of all.

In the meantime, Lee De Forest had been busily at work inventing. The wireless equipment of the time was incredibly primitive, permitting only wireless telegraphy. Transmitters using spark gaps blasted kilowatts of power out over the airwaves. But solid-state radio detectors of the time were so insensitive that they had trouble picking up even these powerful signals.

De Forest concentrated on developing an improved wireless detector in New York in 1903. It wasn't until after he'd made his great invention that he learned what Thomas Alva Edison had discovered more than twenty years before.

In 1883, when Edison was working with carbon filaments in his first successful light bulb design, he noticed that the inside of the glass bulbs gradually became blackened by a deposit of carbon. The film inside the bulb was uniform except for a fine clear line where it seemed the filament support itself cast a "shadow." Edison guessed that the deposit was coming from the carbon filament, but he couldn't explain the shadow. When he built a test lamp with a small metal plate between the two filament support legs, he discovered that the plate drew a small current only when connected to the positive voltage side of the filament, never when connected to the negative side.

After J. J. Thompson discovered the electron in 1896, the forgotten Edison effect was brought to mind by Sir John Ambrose Fleming, one of Edison's assistants who later became professor of electrical engineering at University College in London. Fleming surmised that the hot carbon filament was "boiling off" electrons that were attracted across the intervening vacuum when the plate was charged positive relative to the filament. When the plate carried a negative charge relative to the filament, the electrons were repelled and would not flow. Fleming redesigned Edison's tube, surrounding the filament with a metal wall that was positively charged. This permitted the passage of electrons during the positive half of every cycle of alternating current. Fleming had invented the first electron or vacuum tube, a device that could be considered a "gaseous-state diode," which worked precisely the same way as today's solid-state diode. For decades a diode was, in fact, a vacuum tube.

In 1903, Lee De Forest reinvented the Edison effect and what was called the "Fleming valve." He was looking for a better wireless detector. He planned to let wireless waves ionize the gas inside the bulb (vacuums were not very good in those days) and thereby make the internal resistance between the filament and plate follow the variation in the radio signal. In later years, De Forest's tubes would be considered "gas filled" by a generation of electronic engineers having access to Langmuir's diffusion vacuum pump. To increase the ionizing effect, De Forest wrapped a piece of tin foil around the outside of the bulb and connected it to the receiving antenna. "I then realized," wrote De Forest, "that the efficiency could be still further enhanced if this third electrode were introduced *inside* the bulb." He next realized that this control electrode would be still more effective if he put it *between* the filament and the plate. Then he decided that the electrode would be even better if it were "simply a piece of wire bent back and forth and located as close to the filament as possible."

Thus, the three-electrode vacuum tube, the "triode," was born. It was far superior to any wireless detector of the time, even in its crudest form. It was the prototype of billions of vacuum tubes that have since been built, including the ones that went into the first electronic computers. De Forest made all his experiments in secret, working only at night and keeping his tube, which he called an "audion," in a wax-sealed box with the connections on the outside. When he finally felt he had it working well as a wireless detector, he passed the "cans" (earphones) to an assistant, who was shocked by the power of the incoming signals and shouted: "My God, doc! Hear those signals! What have you got in that box?"

Shortly thereafter, De Forest formed the North American Wireless Company. In 1910, having discovered some of the audio amplification potential of his audion tube, he staged the first musical radio broadcast in history from the Metropolitan Opera House with Enrico Caruso. In 1911, the government began a crusade against wireless stock promoters, and De Forest was caught by the crossfire. Lee De Forest was neither a financier nor a marketing man. He was far more interested in and enamored by technology. Unable to raise funds to further support the development of his audion, De Forest had to put his company into bankruptcy.

He still had his audion and the patent rights for what Nobel laureate I. I. Rabi was later to claim was an invention "ranking with the greatest of all time."

At that point, he'd gone through an unhappy marriage and

two fortunes. A fractious, independent man, he swallowed his pride and took a job as an engineer at $300 a month with a small firm, the Federal Telegraph Company, located in Palo Alto, California.

The Federal Telegraph Company was the oldest American radio firm. It turned out to be a technological nursery much like many other Silicon Valley companies that were to follow in its footsteps. It not only created new products, but also new companies and the bright people who were to run them.

The San Francisco Bay area was a center for people who were interested in the new area of electronics, then called wireless and later "radio." Whereas on the East Coast wireless enthusiasts, professional and amateur, were interested in bridging the Atlantic Ocean to establish regular and reliable wireless contact with Europeans, the people around San Francisco saw wireless as a way to end the relative isolation of the West Coast at that time. California had always been isolated from the rest of America. It took months to travel by ship around Cape Horn before the transcontinental railroad was completed in 1869. Even by railroad, it was a three-day journey to New York and Washington, two days to Chicago. There was no other way to travel. Durea and Ford had yet to come up with the automobiles that would make the trek, and there were no roads to speak of. Early in the twentieth century, airplanes were an unreliable sport for the wealthy, not the people-hauling, long-distance transportation devices of today. Wireless offered an end to this isolation.

Propelled by this, young men living in the Bay Area built the first major wireless radio station, now KCBS in San Francisco. They were the first to demonstrate wireless contact between an airplane in flight and the ground, although H. M. Horton had to go east to accomplish this at an air meet near Sheepshead Bay, New York, on August 27, 1910. The Federal Telegraph Company attracted many of these young wireless wizards and became a dominant force in this infant industry. Among those Federal Telegraph engineers who went on to greater things was Charles Litton, who started giant Litton Industries in a garage in San Carlos, decades ahead of later Silicon Valley millionaires who began in the same way. Former Federal Telegraph employees Peter Jensen and E. S. Pridham invented the loudspeaker and established a firm called Magnavox Company in 1917. Jensen further developed the hi-fi and stereo loudspeakers that still carry his name. Frederick Kolster of Federal Telegraph invented the radio direction finder. Ralph Heintz left Federal Telegraph to form Heintz and Kauffmann in 1921, then built the shortwave radio transmitters used by Rear Admiral Richard E. Byrd in Antarctica.

The proximity of Stanford University helped these inventors. Here was an academic institution that could attract the best brains in the world to do the research that Silicon Valley entrepreneurs would later apply to totally new products in the communication and data-processing industries. For example, Frederick Terman, whose father had developed the famous Stanford-Binet intelligence test (its data was correlated initially by Hollerith's Electric Tabulating Company machinery), took his doctorate at MIT and in 1925 began teaching electrical engineering at Stanford. Terman started the university's radio communications lab and attracted gifted students as the laboratory's fame spread.

But back in 1911, Lee De Forest still had a lot of work to do on his audion tube, and he devoted his time to exploring all its possibilities at the Federal Telegraph Company. Working both at the plant and in his white clapboard house at 913 Emerson Street in Palo Alto, De Forest discovered that the audion tube worked even better as an *amplifier* of electrical signals. A very small change in the voltage applied to the third electrode or grid would cause a large change in the electron flow or current between the hot filament and the positively charged plate. Furthermore, as the grid voltage was changed, the signal at the plate followed it exactly. His method of testing the gain of his amplifier was crude but effective. He would set a loudspeaker in the window of his laboratory and walk away until he couldn't hear it anymore. When he had developed the audion and its circuit enough to give a "two-block gain," he wrote to a friend in New York, John Stone, who got AT&T interested in buying the rights to the audion as a telephone amplifier or "repeater," which would make possible practical long-distance telephone calls.

In the fall of 1913, AT&T paid $50,000 for the telephone repeater rights. In October 1914, the Western Electric Company, which had fired Lee De Forest a little over ten years before, paid him $90,000 for the radio rights and $250,000 for the remaining rights.

Dr. Lee De Forest's triode vacuum tube alone brought the United States and its electronic industry to the forefront of the world's communications industry and produced an industrial base and output that, by 1950, was worth more than $3 billion.

But AT&T, Western Electric, the Federal Telegraph Company, and even Dr. Lee De Forest himself hadn't even guessed at what would eventually become the most striking and useful application of the audion or triode tube.

The tube was not only useful as a radio-frequency detector and an amplifier of both audio and radio frequencies, but was also the world's fastest switch. It was a relay with no moving parts except submicroscopic, almost weightless electrons.

Thirty years later, the triode vacuum tube invented and perfected by Dr. Lee De Forest would make possible the first electronic digital computers.

But the computer had to mature first, and the market for it had to be allowed to develop through two wars, a boom, and a whopping bust of a depression.

7

Ballistics, Bombsights, and Brass Brains

In 1913, Europe was headed inexorably toward war. It might have been stopped or even localized if better communications and modern data processing had been available to both the Allies and the Central Powers. We'll never know, just as we'll never know how many wars have been prevented by today's instant communication and by computers digesting more data in a second than a soldier could in ten years.

What was then called "the Great War" and is now called World War I broke out in Europe in 1914. It was the first computer war. In fact, it was the first large technological war, although the American Civil War had pioneered some of the aspects of this mode of armed conflict. Like the airplane, the computer didn't play a large role in World War I. But, in concert with the airplane, World War I served to stimulate the development and utilization of computers in their early, primitive states.

Although we know the exact moment when World War I began (11:00 A.M., July 28, 1914, when Austria-Hungary notified Serbia that war had been declared), it isn't as easy to pinpoint the exact beginning of certain technical developments associated with computers in that war. Practically all the computer hardware used during the war was already in hand on that summer day in 1914. There were no major developments in computer technology during the war, but computers did play a major role in several events. There were other incidents that didn't seem at the time to have anything to do with computers at all, but often minor historical footnotes can lead to unforeseen consequences of major importance at a later time.

Many of the principles of automation—the application of logical automata to industrial processes in the second industrial revolution (see Chapters 2 and 6)—came from widely variant fields of activity. Many of them were war oriented. They could make a good case for any researcher, graduate student, or historian seeking examples of turning swords into plowshares. The early years of the technology involved with making automatic machines were happy ones for young, creative engineers and inventors, as is true in most infant, emerging technologies.

One such fecund inventor was Elmer Ambrose Sperry (1860-1930). He became interested in machinery, he later said, as a result of a visit to the Centennial Exhibition in Philadelphia in 1876. Sperry decided to become an engineer. So he spent a year at Cornell University, grew disinterested with studies and bored by academia, and invented an improved dynamo and arc lamp in 1879. On his twentieth birthday, he opened the Sperry Electric Company factory in Chicago to manufacture his inventions. He became interested in mining and formed the Sperry Electric Mining Company in 1888. His interest in electricity and machinery, especially the then-new diesel engines, led him to form the Sperry Electric Railway Company in 1890 and the National Battery Company. His wide-ranging interests also encompassed chemical engineering and what we would today term the recycling technologies. In 1900, with C. F. Townsend, he organized a research laboratory in Washington, D.C., where he developed a process for making pure caustic soda (sodium hydroxide) from salt, as well as a process for recovering tin from used cans and scrap.

While watching his children play with a toy gyroscope in about 1896, Elmer Sperry became interested in the gyro's ability to maintain its orientation.

A gyro is a spinning top. It will keep its axis of spin pointed in a given direction as long as it is kept spinning. A toy top is started by pulling a string wrapped around it, and there's no way to keep it going afterward. A gyro, on the other hand, is kept spinning usually by a jet of air impinging on little scoops machined into the outer circumference of the gyro rotor or wheel. When an outside force is applied to the axis of a spinning gyro, it behaves strangely. It doesn't push back the way Sir Isaac Newton said things should (the Third Law of Motion)—"for every acting force there is an equal and oppositely directed reacting force." The reaction is at *right angles* to the applied force.

Curl your right hand into a semifist with your index finger pointed away from you, your thumb pointed at right angles to the left, and your fingers curled in a counterclockwise direction when viewed from over your thumb. This is the "right hand rule" of gyros. If the rotor is spinning counterclockwise in the direction your fingers are curled, and if the applied force is in the direction your index finger is pointing, the gyro will react by tipping at right angles to the left, the direction your thumb is pointing. This behavior is indeed strange, and scientists have been trying to explain it for over a hundred years. Technologists, however, often don't wait until scientists explain why; they go ahead and use the phenomenon anyway.

Elmer Sperry did just that. If the axis of a gyro remained fixed in space and if it reacted when disturbed. Sperry figured that he could harness this phenomenon to provide foolproof guidance for ships.

Holding course with a magnetic compass wasn't much of a problem when ships were made of wood. But the new steel "dreadnaught" battleships were the national airlines, Main Battle Tanks, and Concorde SSTs of the day. Every government aspiring to the title of "world-class power" had to have one or more dreadnaughts, including such nations as Brazil and Argentina, whose national treasuries were drained by the expense of these huge vessels. One of their many technical problems was stability and reliability of the primary navigational instrument, the magnetic compass. When a gun turret was turned, the ship's magnetic compass could be deflected by as much as 25 degrees. The first practical solution to this was a gyrocompass patented in 1908 by Dr. Herman Anschutz-Kaempfe. It was merely a substitute for the magnetic compass and was a huge affair that occupied a large amount of deck space on the bridge of a ship.

Elmer Sperry went one better. With his associate Hannibal Ford, he improved the Anschutz gyro. He perfected the "repeater" gyrocompass, a device that allowed the gyro itself to be placed in the best location in the ship and a "repeater" or remote read-out device to be installed where it was needed on the bridge. One of these was installed on the S.S. *Princess Anne* in 1911.

Beyond that, Elmer Sperry linked his gyrocompass directly to the steering rudder. Any deviation from a preset course would be detected by the gyro, which would cause the rudder to be activated to correct the ship's direction back to the intended course. This is an early application of the feedback principle vital to the technology of automation and to the self-programming and self-correcting computers of the late twentieth century. These first gyro-controlled autopilots were initially installed in naval torpedoes, immediately increasing the effective range by a factor of more than two. Because these early gyro autopilots didn't take *rate* of change into account and therefore produced an *overcorrection,* they steered torpedoes toward their targets in a series of sinuous curves.

The application of this technology to the carnage of submarine warfare had another side—a lifesaving application. In 1909, Elmer Sperry and Hannibal Ford designed and installed the first gyroscopic stabilizer in an airplane. This was the direct ancestor of the device that today safely guides thousands of airplanes through the skies every day. It contained gyros to sense the pitch, roll, and yaw axes. These gyros worked the control surfaces through remote actuators called servomotors— motors that were "slaved" to the gyro outputs and therefore served the gyros, moving only when the gyros told them to. But Sperry faced a more difficult problem than he'd solved in applying gyro control to naval torpedoes: a correction needed at one air speed might make the airplane crash at another and shed its wings at yet another. He solved the problem by connecting the gyro stabilizing system to an air-speed indicator, which modified the force of the servomotors and hence the deflection of the control surfaces, depending upon the airplane's speed. Here again was the early application of an important principle of automation: sensing not only the performance of the machine, but elements of its environment as well.

Early in 1914, the Aero Club de France sponsored an

international competition for a safe airplane with a prize of fifty thousand francs. Elmer's son, Lawrence Sperry, entered a Curtiss biplane equipped with the Sperry gyroscopic stabilizer. As he flew by the judges' stand, he stood up and waved both arms. At the same time, his 170-pound mechanic walked six feet out on one wing, severely unbalancing the craft. But the wings stayed absolutely level, and the frail Curtiss airplane maintained its original course and altitude. Needless to say, this was a convincing demonstration. Lawrence Sperry won the prize.

It was the first success of Sperry's first computer.

It also paved the way for the first automatic bombsights, which matured during World War II into the famous Norden bombsight. This not only computed and corrected for the falling trajectory of a bomb, but also took control of the aircraft during the bomb run when it was computing. No other nation had a device comparable to the Norden machine.

But whereas Sperry's invention of the gyrocompass, gyro autopilot, and gyro stabilizer permitted submarines to hold their courses more accurately and extended the range of torpedoes, another development of early computer technology provided a countermeasure.

Tidal prediction is an extremely complex problem. Even when the distance of the sun is known, the distance of the moon determinable, and the position of the moon in its wobbling orbit also known, the physiography and topography of the earth itself interacts to affect the tides in a given locale. There are also land tides. True, they are small, amounting to only an inch or less. And there are straits, inlets, bays, harbors, capes, and other irregularities in coastlines. All of these factors interact. There are some locations in the world—Long Island Sound, for example—where tidal prediction had almost been a matter of guesswork because of restrictions to the tidal inflow and outflow of seawater through Hell Gate on the west and the convoluted and complex topography of Block Island Sound on the east.

Predicting tides is not a problem today. A large main-frame computer can do it for anyplace in the entire world in an hour or so. But before World War I, tidal prediction was an art, not a science.

It did respond to computational analysis by machine, however. In 1899, E. G. Fischer and R. A. Harris at the U.S. Coast and Geodetic Survey began the development of a tide-predicting machine. By 1914, it was ready for work. *Scientific American* called it "the great brass brain." It was mechanical, as all computers were in those days, but it was a tremendous improvement over previous machines. Basically, it was a harmonic integrator. It could handle thirty-seven tidal components, most of them in sine wave form. These thirty-seven sine wave components were mechanically added together by the machine to produce a tide chart. The results were displayed on dials.

The tidal data from the great brass brain saved lives during World War I—Allied ships could maneuver safely into, through, and around shallow water, shoals, tidal banks, and reefs. German submarines couldn't because the U-boat skippers didn't have that tidal data and ran the risk of going aground while submerged. When the Germans found out about the great brass brain, they built one of their own and installed it in the Imperial Observatory in 1916. Now that both sides had the same data, the game was square again, and the matter of gaining the initiative passed on to other technologies.

World War I was the first general war in which enormous numbers of people were involved, all industrial areas became important, and millions of soldiers were put into the field. Statistical analysis by machine, pioneered by Hollerith, Powers, Felt, and others between 1890 and 1914, became an absolutely necessary tool of the warring governments.

Although the United States didn't become an active belligerent in World War I until April 1917, the government began to utilize machine-generated statistical analysis and data processing beyond the limited scope of the Bureau of the Census in 1913. The nation was growing, and there was also a growing political philosophy exemplified by the Wilson administration that the federal government should become far more involved in social matters. To carry out these newly adopted social functions, it needed to have rapid access to much information and the ability to tabulate and analyze it quickly.

America's entry into World War I on April 6, 1917, forced the Wilson administration, under war powers authority, to establish controls over all American industry. Government agencies were quickly established to control transportation and communications for the benefit of the war effort. Other agencies, boards, bureaus, and committees were set up to regulate production and distribution from factories, mines, and farms. There was a de facto nationalization of railroads. The most powerful, all-encompassing wartime control agency was the War Industries Board, under the chairmanship of the noted financier Bernard M. Baruch. It virtually took over the industrial infrastructure of the United States. There were committees for ice, biscuits and crackers, pocketknives, photographs, cars, baby buggies, candy, elevators, and foundry supplies. The purpose of this huge, centralized bureaucracy was to marshal the industrial might of America to win a war. Not since the Civil War had the nation been so totally mobilized for war.

This involved a massive data-processing job. The War Industries Board never really had the time to get everything completely set up. Not only was there little time between April 1917 and November 1918, but there was a shortage of tabulating and sorting equipment to handle the job. Even at that, scores of subordinate committees and boards collected information and fed it into the War Industries Board. For the first time in the nation's history there was a semicomprehensive picture of the total industrial capacity available.

To add to this massive data-processing task, Congress passed the conscription law in May 1917. Two of the biggest problems of wartime mobilization turned out to be putting draftees into uniforms that fit and putting those same draftees into jobs they could do.

This first problem seems trivial today. But in 1917, nobody knew how big the American people were. Even mail-order clothing available from Sears, Roebuck and Company was almost custom-made from measurements of the customer sent along with the order. Most off-the-rack clothing was ill-fitting. If clothing fit a person, it usually meant that the wearer could afford the services of a tailor. In spite of a huge clothing industry, the United States Army didn't know how many uniforms of different sizes to order. As a result, they had to measure draftees to get a data base. During World War I, more than a hundred thousand men were measured to get data for sizing uniforms. Twenty-three measurements were taken. This yielded more than twenty-three million pieces of data. Hollerith's C-T-R Company sorting and tabulating machines were used to correlate this information into the very first picture of the size and weight of American men. (True to stereotype, Texans were the tallest. Men from Alaska were heaviest. The men from North Dakota had the largest chests.)

This anthropometric (man measurement) data was taken and processed too late to be of much use in clothing the American doughboy. If the uniforms of Yank soldiers of World War I look ill-fitting in old photographs, it is simply because they were. It led to endless jokes about uniform sizes, which were perpetuated well into World War II, because even at that late date the Army Quartermaster Corps ignored the most important factor in the data: the "normal curve" of distribution. Although the Quartermaster Corps knew the various sizes of men, they didn't use the data properly during the interwar years. At the start of World War II, they provided the Army Air Corps pilots at Wright-Patterson Field in Ohio with coveralls in ten sizes, 10 percent in each size.

The Army also faced another problem that wasn't totally solved in either World War I or II. America was no longer a nation of farmers and tradesmen. The Morrill Land Grant Act of 1862 had resulted in the establishment of dozens of colleges of agriculture and mechanic arts (the state A & M schools) throughout the nation. By 1917, many Americans had a high school education and there were a large number of college-educated people, especially in the professions of medicine and law. These specialized talents had to be properly utilized because the Army realized that it must conserve brainpower. Unlike the European nations, which sent the pride of their manhood to die in the mud of no-man's land, the American government wanted to mobilize quickly into an effective force and knew that proper utilization of manpower was the key to doing it.

The United States Army conducted the first large-scale psychological testing in order to properly and efficiently use its manpower in the shortest possible time. Edward L. Thorndike, a pioneer in applying psychological testing to the learning process, headed the Army's wartime statistical unit. Not only did this organization serve as an important laboratory for experienced psychologists who were able for the first time to get measurements on a very large sample, but it also served as a training ground for up-and-coming young psychologists. The Committee on Developing Methods of Psychological Examination in 1917 was headed by Major Robert M. Yerkes and included some of the top psychologists and statisticians in the country. They had some early work to rely on as a foundation. French psychologist Alfred Binet, the director of the then-new psychological laboratory at the Sorbonne in Paris, had been the first to apply the mathematics of statistics to measuring mental capabilities in 1908. This had been expanded by the work of Frederick Terman and his colleagues at Stanford University.

Two tests were designed by Yerkes to discover special skills and leadership capabilities of interest to the Army. These tests were also designed to identify recruits who would likely be useless or even dangerous under battle conditions. The Alpha test was given to draftees who could read, whereas the Beta test was designed for illiterates.

Psychologist H. H. Goddard recalled: "We worked out material for the Test of Common Sense, including such problems as whether cows have horns because we need horn in the art of making combs, because they add beauty and dignity to the appearance of the cow, for protection, or because our grandfathers used them for powder horns. Also a series of disarranged sentences such as 'Hell to with Bill Kaiser.' "

The results were coded onto Hollerith cards using C-T-R equipment. This project wasn't as much of a "too little and too late" affair as was measuring the physical size of draftees. It might have taken years to correlate the data, but because of the tabulating and sorting machines, the Army was able to fill such specialized personnel requirements as 150 theatrical scene painters whom they put to work on camouflage nets and 600 chauffeurs who spoke French.

Although all this was done to satisfy wartime needs, the methods and procedures developed for such anthropological requirements form the basis for nearly all our modern techniques of marketing. Without the computers of the time, primitive and slow as they were, this new field might never have opened up or at least not until years later.

World War I provided an extremely firm foundation for the budding computer industry by demonstrating the need for and the value of information handling and processing. America's pivotal role in World War I, and later in World War II, was not just a matter of sheer industrial might. Power can be frittered away and wasted if it isn't properly applied or directed. Americans were outstanding *managers* of their industrial power and resources because they had better information upon which to base their decisions. And this was due to computers and data processing.

The American obsession with efficiency far outstripped the fabled and legendary German propensity for thoroughness and "scientific" application of resources. This became evident in World War I, but it was ignored. The stereotyped highly efficient German continued to maintain this image until Americans demolished it thoroughly in World War II. Nowhere was it more in evidence than at the U.S. Army's Aberdeen Proving Ground in Maryland during World War I in an activity that wasn't prominent then and was therefore forgotten until the computer giants produced there began to surface a quarter of a century later.

The years prior to World War I had produced new kinds of artillery and ammunition. World War I's static war fronts intensified these developments. The emergence of large-caliber guns on battleships and later on wheeled or railway mounts for land use created new problems for gunners. When the range of guns was extended, the shells were lofted high into the thin upper atmosphere of the earth. Air resistance on the shells was decreased. As a result, some of these large-caliber guns fired shells that went as much as twice the distance anticipated. The new field of antiaircraft artillery (known then as "Archie" and later as "flak") required enormous accuracy, and the old-fashioned methods of computing range tables broke down completely when these high-velocity shells were fired vertically up through an atmosphere that grew thinner with increasing altitude.

In the leisurely years of peace, guns could be tested and retested on artillery ranges to determine how far a shell would go with a certain powder load and gun-barrel elevation as a function of air temperature around the gun at the time of firing. These tests produced "ballistic tables," which would tell gunners how to aim their artillery pieces to hit an unseen target miles away. The exigencies of war made it impossible to engage in lengthy tests, even on the battlefield. Shells had to land where intended lest they fall on friendly troops or harmlessly in vacant fields.

The U.S. Army called in the experts in mathematical analyses. They hired University of Chicago astronomer Professor Forest Ray Moulton as Chief of Ordnance. In a tract entitled *New Methods in Exterior Ballistics,* Moulton had developed mathematical equations of motion that were capable of giving a numerical solution to projectile trajectories. In later years, *Ordnance* magazine pointed out, Moulton "uprooted the forest of empiricism and planted in its place the seed of massive calculations."

In the absence of large main-frame, number-crunching computers, a large cadre of mathematicians was required. Moulton brought in Princeton mathematician Oswald Veblen. As Major Veblen, he was responsible for assembling a group of university mathematicians at Aberdeen Proving Ground to further apply scientific techniques to the preparation of precise gunnery tables. Veblen created and managed research programs that paralleled theory with wind-tunnel experiments and proving-ground tests. The Aberdeen work, even in the short space of about a year, dramatically improved the precision of gunnery tables. Veblen's command prepared mathematically precise tables of gun and ammunition types, map data, powder-charge temperature, and such meteorological data as air temperature and density and wind velocity.

Among the mathematicians brought to Aberdeen was a young prodigy, Norbert Weiner. Born in Columbia, Missouri, in 1894, he attended Tufts College and received his Ph.D. in mathematics from Harvard University at the age of eighteen.

In his book *Ex-prodigy,* Weiner recalls the intellectual conditions at Aberdeen during the war years: "When we were not working on the noisy hand-computing machines which we knew as 'crashers', we were playing bridge together and using the same computing machines to record our scores." Thus, things have not changed greatly in the departments of mathematics, engineering, and number crunching.

In the same book Weiner observes: "For many years after the war, the overwhelming majority of significant American mathematicians was to be found among those who had gone through the discipline of the Proving Ground."

Wartime needs breed strange and apparently disconnected

progeny. In spite of its violence and slaughter, war produces both new technical developments and people who will work during peacetime to improve the human condition. World War I brought no computer breakthroughs, but it did generate new applications of existing hardware and create a cadre of people to insure the continuation of the computer revolution.

8

"Men, Minutes, Money"

The man who undoubtedly was the driving force behind the computer revolution was Thomas J. Watson, Sr., followed closely by his son, Thomas J. Watson, Jr. The elder Watson (who we'll be talking about for the rest of this chapter) not only foresaw many of the benefits of computers back in the days when they were whirring, clanking mechanical monsters, but he also knew how to *sell* computer equipment. Having a new technical miracle is one thing, but turning it into a product and getting people to buy and use it are just as important. Furthermore, Watson encouraged others to find new applications for computers and generously supported these researchers with outright gifts of computer equipment.

Thomas J. Watson was born in Campbell, New York, in 1874. He learned about money and salesmanship early in life. At the age of eighteen, he began work as a bookkeeper in a grocery store, then went on to sell sewing machines and musical instruments. He may well have served as the prototype for Professor Harold Hill in *The Music Man*, although Watson was no con-artist salesman. He went to work for John H. Patterson's National Cash Register Company in Dayton, Ohio. Within nine years, he'd become the general sales manager of that company.

Watson undoubtedly learned a great deal from Patterson's basic business philosophy and company policies. Whether Watson created some of these sales policies or simply implemented and perhaps improved upon Patterson's basic ideas is impossible to know. Patterson is credited with debunking the theory that "salesmen are born, not made" because he began to train salesmen and establish incentives for performance. Among the new sales techniques pioneered by the National Cash Register Company during Watson's tenure with the firm:

- Sales agents were given exclusive territories based on Patterson's marketing data that a cash register could be sold for every four hundred citizens.
- Sales point systems were established along with monthly and annual sales quotas.
- Based on this point system, the Century Point Club (CPC) was established for outstanding salesmen.
- Exceptional sales performance was rewarded by incentive programs involving special prizes, trips, and conventions.
- In the late 1880s, the National Cash Register Company placed heavy emphasis on direct mail advertising to support its field sales force.
- Formal sales training was established in 1890.
- The NCR Primer, a handbook containing a word-for-word sales presentation to be memorized by all salesmen, was written and published.

These methods were all new to salesmanship. The Saturday Evening Post reported: "Patterson changed the cigar-puffing whiskey-reeking salesmen into a new breed of men."

Patterson also pioneered in the area of employee welfare and incentives. The idea that employees were valuable company assets was practically unheard of at the time. In order to improve quality control, Patterson had all NCR factories rebuilt "with as much glass as structurally possible" to admit light and fresh air into production areas. He installed shower baths, bathrooms, medical dispensaries, water fountains, lunch rooms, and exercise facilities. He was the first industrialist to establish an employee suggestion system. He urged employees to submit their ideas for improving products and business operations.

Watson is often thought of as the man who installed "THINK!" signs everywhere. But it was Patterson who came up with this idea and had the "THINK!" signs posted in all NCR facilities in the 1890s.

Many of his contemporaries in other companies considered John H. Patterson to be a "radical" and even a dangerous man for espousing his ideas of employee welfare and actually putting them into practice. They began to change their minds, albeit slowly, when Patterson's ideas began to work and some took these concepts with them to other firms. Thus, the early computer industry had a pivotal role in the development of modern management techniques, as well as the miracle machines that made work easier.

Thomas J. Watson was on the ground floor of the development of the new profession of sales and the new management techniques that were far in advance of "Theory Y" and other later management practices. Whatever part he played in the development of these "firsts" is inconsequential to what he did with them later.

In 1911, industrialist Charles R. Flint had engineered one of the most far-reaching mergers in the history of the computer industry. He brought together under a single management Hollerith's Tabulating Machine Company with the Computing Scale Company and the International Time Recording Company. The new corporate entity became known as the Computing-Tabulating-Recording Company, or C-T-R for short. In 1914, Flint convinced Thomas J. Watson to leave NCR and join C-T-R as the new general manager.

This great motivator of people began to motivate in earnest now that he was totally responsible for the operations of the infant C-T-R company. One of Watson's first acts was to codify three basic company policies. They sound commonplace today, but they were new ideas in 1914:

1. Profit for customers.
2. Profit for employees.
3. Profit for stockholders.

The priority was in that order as well, for Watson believed that if his customers made a profit with C-T-R products, the market would expand. If the market expanded, production would have to be increased. Production increase depended upon employees, and the necessary level of quality control couldn't be maintained if the employees were overworked and did not participate in the success of the company. And, if the customers and the employees were profiting from success, the stockholders would in turn profit in terms of increased dividends and improvement of the market price of their stock holdings.

At that time, C-T-R had 770 stockholders and the stock was worth $30 a share. By the end of 1914, there were 1,346 C-T-R employees and gross income had risen to $4 million. Hollerith's original factory in Washington, D.C., was making tabulating and sorting machines, as well as printing punch cards. The plant in Endicott, New York, was producing time clocks and other time-recording equipment. In Dayton, Ohio, the C-T-R factory made computing scales. C-T-R headquarters was located at 50 Broad Street in New York City.

But it takes time to accomplish things in any organization simply because it takes time to make things change. Just like a large mass, an organization has inertia. It wasn't until 1915 that Watson really began to hit his stride. In that year, Watson was elected both president and general manager, giving him the power to carry his plans even further. The new chairman of the board was George Fairchild, a man who backed Watson all the way and who later was instrumental in forming the Fairchild Camera and Instrument Company.

Watson, a man with little formal education, nevertheless understood the value of education. "There is no saturation point in education," he stated. In 1916 he established the first school to educate his sales force about the company's products and to familiarize them with new products. He organized the first sales convention in history, the forerunner of the famous Hundred Percent Club conventions and of the thousands of sales conventions held around the world every year.

But Watson went further than just encouraging and educating his salesmen. He also set up the first company educational program for every employee and a department to run it. The program was later expanded to include company classes in sales, customer engineering, and manufacturing. This was all part of the three basic company policies he'd announced in 1914 when he became general manager.

Product development and company research and development were other principles that Watson brought with him from

NCR. In 1914, C-T-R's basic Hollerith tabulating machine was renting for $150 per month. The company's main competition was the rival Powers Company, which had arisen from the Census Bureau's earlier desire to build its own tabulators and the subsequent decision of their engineer, Powers, to form his own company. The Powers Company was renting their machine for only $100 a month, and it offered features such as the ability to automatically print its results.

Watson openly challenged two of his engineers to a contest to invent a competitive machine. Clair Lake came up with the winner, a tabulator with a printing attachment. At the 1919 sales convention, Watson introduced it from the stage with appropriate flourishes. He threw a switch and the machine began tabulating and printing its results. The salesmen stood on their chairs and cheered.

The year 1920 not only saw the introduction of this new printing tabulator, but also the C-T-R Company in the Canadian market (where it had been incorporated as International Business Machines Company, Ltd., the first use of that name in the company), as well as in France. The number of employees had risen to more than three thousand. The company's gross annual income had *tripled* since 1914.

Watson continued with his educational efforts. In 1920, he established an executive training school at Shawnee-on-Delaware, Pennsylvania and began putting all the firm's executives through a five-day management course.

"You make a business grow," Watson proclaimed, "when you begin growing men!"

He kept at it. At every sales meeting, every sales convention, and every opening session of the growing number of company schools, he exhorted the employees. His oratory was peppered with morale-boosting slogans to give his people confidence in themselves and the company's products. The company collected his speeches and published them in a booklet, the title of which was taken from one of Watson's favorite talks, *Men, Minutes, Money!* The C-T-R sales rooms and factories were billboards not only for the famous "THINK!" sign he had borrowed from NCR, but others such as:

"STUDY!"
"LEARN!"

"ANALYZE YOURSELF."

"DON'T GUESS—KNOW."

"MEN MAKE THE BUSINESS."

"THE BEST SUPERVISION IS SELF-SUPERVISION."

"ALL MEN SHOULD BE JUDGED UPON THEIR RECORDS."

"THE GREATEST TEACHER IN THE WORLD IS YOURSELF."

"THINK IN BIG FIGURES."

"PROGRESS IS IMPROVEMENT."

These signs might draw chuckles in today's more sophisticated business environment, but the rationale behind them is still valid.

Other companies, not only competitors, had to follow suit because Watson's concepts *worked*. And there's nothing as persuasive in the competitive business world as an idea that works. The Soviet Union picked up the idea, but couldn't implement the self-motivation element that made Watson's approach so effective. Following World War II, the Japanese also discovered Watson's work and improved upon his basic motivational discoveries. Watson the salesman knew what made people tick: any arrangement that offered and produced a way to better the lot of the individual person and his family.

There were competitors for the C-T-R Company, but they had trouble competing against what was then an enormous power in the computer industry.

In 1925, the company paid its *first* stock dividend at a rate of 20 percent; it had taken sixteen years to come from Flint's original combination to profitability. But Watson was not through. There was more he wanted to do with computing machinery.

That was evident in 1924, when the Computing-Tabulating-Recording Company changed its name to International Business Machines Corporation. IBM (later to be nicknamed "Big Blue" because of the color of its corporate logo) had been born, and it was the biggest, most powerful baby the world had ever seen. True, General Motors and other companies were bigger at the time, but they could not match IBM's huge potential.

IBM kept right on growing and improving its products. In 1928, the requirements for increased data processing resulted in the Hollerith card (subsequently misnamed the IBM card) being redesigned to hold eighty columns of punched data, doubling its capacity. High-speed rotary presses had been developed to produce these cards in huge quantities.

Even when the stock market crashed in 1929, IBM declared a 5 percent stock dividend and its gross income passed the $18 million mark. In the wake of this Wall Street disaster, which quickly spread to become a worldwide economic epidemic, Watson managed to keep the faith. He sincerely believed not only in his own product, but also in salesmanship as a profession. During the depths of the depression, he did something no other company dared do: he hired more salesmen. When criticized about this by business contemporaries, he remarked wryly: "Well, you know when a man gets about my age, he always does something foolish. Some men play too much poker, and others bet on horse races, and one thing and another. My bet's on more salesmen."

Watson's unusual actions were undoubtedly due to his vision of what computers would eventually be capable of accomplishing for people. He also had good demographic and other marketing input. For example, he was informed in 1929 that only 2 percent of the bookkeeping and accounting in American industry was done by machinery. His reaction: "Think of that! I haven't been able to get that statement out of my mind since I read it. Two per cent! Think of the field we have to work upon."

Another reason for Watson's greatness and for IBM's continuing lead in the computer industry was his early enthusiasm for supporting research and utilization of IBM's machinery outside the company's R&D programs and beyond its usual business markets. An excellent example of this was Watson's willingness to help Ben D. Wood, a psychologist at Columbia University.

Benjamin Dekalbe Wood had an extensive background in education when he came to Columbia as an instructor in 1921. He was also an experimenter who was interested in the application of various new machines and concepts for improving educational processes. He was among the first educators to experiment with typewriters and motion pictures in the classroom as an integral part of schoolwork. As he continued his studies, however, Wood became more and more Kelvinian in his thinking.

The term "Kelvinian" derives from the British mathematician and physicist Lord Kelvin (William Thompson) (1824-1907), who stated in 1886: "I often say that when you can measure something and express it in numbers, you know something about it. But when you cannot measure it, when you cannot express it in numbers, your knowledge is of a meager and unsatisfactory kind; it may be the beginning of knowledge, but you have scarcely, in your thoughts, progressed to the level of science, regardless of what the matter may be."

Wood's teacher and mentor, the psychologist E. L. Thorndike, had impressed on his students his belief that "whatever exists at all, exists in some amount." In essence, he was saying the same thing as Lord Kelvin: measurement is the basis for all scientific study.

As a result of this background, Benjamin Wood became interested in the statistical aspects of education. He was well aware of the intellectual testing efforts of Binet and the follow-up work at Stanford University. But he felt more data were required in order to establish a foundation for discovering how much a person could learn as a function of what he or she was mentally equipped to learn.

He set out in 1928 to prepare "an academic inventory of the baccalaureate mind." This was basically a statistical task—gathering and correlating massive amounts of data from a wide variety of sources in order to be assured of working with an adequate statistical universe. The job required that Wood design a battery of tests similar in many respects to the Stanford-Binet I.Q. tests, but targeted instead toward finding out what the testee knew. It was obvious that these tests would have to cover a large number of areas of human knowledge and would have to be given to large numbers of people. It would quickly become a project primarily involved with data management. Wood knew he'd need tabulating and sorting equipment.

He persuaded Thomas J. Watson to "lend" him three truckloads of IBM card-punching, tabulating, and sorting equipment to set up what was to become the Columbia Statistical Bureau, the first university laboratory for educational statistics. Watson not only donated the equipment, but instructed his IBM engineers to help Wood and his people modify it as needed for the task. And modify it they did. In order to enable the tabulator to do the difficult mathematical operations required for the analysis of the educational and psychological tests developed by the

Columbia Statistical Bureau, IBM engineers came up with a key device they called an "emitter." This enabled a total from any of the tabulating and sorting machine registers to be copied into any of the other nine statistical registers of the Columbia machine. This device was so large and impressive that it was nicknamed the "Packard" after the luxury automobile of the time. Even with the IBM machines, it was a long and involved process. By 1938, Wood had analyzed the test scores of 26,548 Pennsylvania high-school seniors under a grant from the Carnegie Foundation for the Advancement of Teaching and published the results in a landmark paper, "The Student and His Knowledge."

Wood's Columbia Statistical Bureau went on to tackle a variety of problems for others. For example, the Bureau's IBM statistical machines were put to work for the university's astronomy department, working out stellar statistics, planetary motions, and star catalogs.

Tranferring test data to punch cards that the IBM machinery could read was still a tedious job. In the early 1930s, Reynold B. Johnson, working in the Michigan school system, invented a machine that could sense handwritten pencil marks on a sheet of paper. A special pencil whose mark would conduct an electric current had to be used to mark the test sheet. Some readers may remember taking tests that used this technology.

The Johnson invention came to the attention of Ben Wood, who in turn showed it to Watson. It was obvious to both men that this was the breakthrough invention that would permit large-scale academic testing. Watson also saw it as the payoff from the early support of Wood's work and a huge expansion of the market for IBM equipment. He hired Reynold Johnson, who helped develop the first commercial test scoring machine, the IBM 805, which became available in 1935.

Millions of students who have suffered through SATs and other academic tests can blame IBM, Watson, Wood, and Johnson for their successes or failures in making qualifying scores for the colleges and universities of their choice. But, just as the early anthropometric work by the U.S. Army Quartermaster Corps in World War I laid the foundation for better-fitting clothing, so the work of the Columbia Statistical Bureau laid a similar intellectual foundation by measuring and analyzing educational factors. Thus, although the early mechanical computers of the 1930s began what seemed to many people to be the "dehumanization" of people, they also helped people discover what a human being really is.

As computing machines became more ubiquitous in the late 1920s and 1930s, the lurking fear that "machines are taking over" began to be more openly and widely expressed. However, few of these expressions of concern were viewed as scenarios in which options and their consequences could be investigated or "modeled" in advance. They were presented and accepted because of their shock value.

Much of this came from the introduction of early automation equipment in factories. The massing of technological know-how and capabilities required to fight World War I was still fresh in people's minds. Samuel Butler's earlier expressions of concern in *Erewhon* and the Frankenstein story were suddenly viewed as alarming possibilities rather than as entertainment. In the 1930s, the suspicions of the apparent dominance, power, and potential human misuse of technology first became a common theme in books, motion pictures, and stage plays.

The word *robot* comes from the Czech language and means drudgery, forced labor, or servitude, depending on the context in which it's used. Robots were unleashed upon the intellectual world by the Czech writer Karel Capek, whose classic stage play *R.U.R.* was first performed in Prague in 1921. It came to America as a Theater Guild Production at the Garrick Theater in New York in 1923. R.U.R. was the corporate entity of the play, Rossum's Universal Robots, makers of what we'd term "androids," or artificial human workers, capable of taking over all the hard work and drudgery of the world. In the play, humans lose control over their creations, the robots, who revolt and destroy humanity, save for the character Alquist, who speaks lines echoing the romantic beliefs of those who have never had to plow the south forty behind a mule: "There was something *good* in service and something *great* in humility. There was some kind of virtue in *toil* and *weariness*." We hear these words paraphrased today by those who fear the computer.

Fritz Lang, the great German motion picture director, was best known for his prescient science fiction movie *The Woman in the Moon (Frau Im Mond)*. But his 1927 picture *Metropolis* dealt with the possibility of domination of people by machines. He, too, utilized the robot. In this case, it was perhaps the most beautiful robot yet to appear in films and was far more attractive than R2D2 or C3PO. The robot Maria stands as a work of art even today. Lang speaks through his robotics scientist, Rotwang: "I have created a machine in the image of man, that never tires or makes a mistake. Now we have no further use for living workers."

Other films portrayed the automated, mechanized future, but missed the fact that the computer was and continues to be a tool. Charlie Chaplin's *Modern Times* and René Clair's *A Nous la Liberté* showed the factory turning humans into robots. How different reality turned out to be, especially when one walks through an automated petroleum refinery.

Aldous Huxley's *Brave New World,* published in 1932, opens with a quote from Nicholas Berdiaeff: "Utopias now appear much more realizable than one used to think. We are now faced with a very different new worry: How to prevent their realization!"

Thus, even while Thomas J. Watson and his contemporaries were hard at work creating a totally different sort of world, people who had no concept of what was being created were starting to voice their opposition to it. This negative reaction has continued. What has also continued is the development of computers by people who believe that no human being should do work that can be done by a machine, that human beings are something more than the robots they created.

The concerns that surfaced in the 1930s continue to be concerns of those who do not understand what is happening in the great transition that is at the heart of the computer revolution.

As for the computer builders in the 1930s, they hadn't even really gotten started yet!

9

The Electrons Take Over

Although computers had progressed from the original Babbage steam-powered "difference engine" to the electrically operated tabulating and sorting equipment of a century later, all computers and calculating machines up to 1940 were basically mechanical in nature. They used gears, levers, cams, and switches. Although many computers used electrical relays, a relay is basically nothing more than an electrically operated mechanical switch. Computers and calculators were electrical in the sense that they were powered by electric motors, although many were operated by means of a hand crank or lever as late as 1960. But they weren't electronic.

These mechanical computers suffered from four basic problems:

1. As their capabilities grew, so did their size.
2. Their speed of operation was limited by the mass and inertia of their mechanical components.
3. The electrical power required to operate them increased rapidly as size increased; since there's always wasted energy that cannot be used in any system and usually appears as heat, the bigger they got, the hotter they got.
4. The presence of mechanical parts moving rapidly against one another or on bearings caused wear and tear, which demanded a great deal of maintenance by

mechanics. Many mechanical repair technicians were and are highly skilled, but there's always been a shortage of maintenance people and therefore many shortcomings in their training and abilities.

This is not to say that mechanical-based computers weren't accurate or suitable for the tasks they were called upon to do during the 1930s.

Dr. Vannevar Bush built his famous "differential analyzer" in 1930 to solve complex equations associated with failures or power blackouts in electrical power networks. It was a mass of cams and turning shafts and electrical contacts. He built similar machines for Aberdeen Proving Ground and the Moore School in Philadelphia. They were all accurate to within plus or minus 0.05 percent.

Nor was extreme dimensional precision required as technical know-how grew. In the summer of 1933, British physicist Douglas R. Hartree used Bush's differential analyzer at MIT and, upon his return to England, decided to build one of his own with his colleague Arthur Porter. Using about $80 worth of Meccano parts—the equivalent to the American Erector sets— Hartree's first demonstration model was accurate within 2 percent. So he used it to solve some extremely complex problems in quantum mechanics!

In 1936, Konrad Zuse built a relay-based calculator in his Berlin apartment with no knowledge of what was being done in England or the United States. All his machines were destroyed during World War II, but he had independently pioneered the use of binary arithmetic, floating decimal point programming, and program control by punched tape. His programs, including his "plan calculus" program, which was a forerunner of modern programming languages, were punched into discarded 35-millimeter motion picture film.

Insofar as being able to do the jobs given to them, the mechanical computers were adequate if enough of them were used. The biggest bookkeeping task in the world began with the passage and signing of the Social Security Act of 1935. This law, championed by President Franklin D. Roosevelt, made it necessary for the federal government to keep employment records of more than twenty-six million people. As the years went by, the number increased. But just to get started, the Social Security

Administration (SSA) had to rent 120,000 square feet of floor space in a Baltimore, Maryland, factory building chosen because it was structurally capable of supporting the weight of 415 card-punch and sorting machines. A production line was set up to punch, sort, check, collate, and file a half million Hollerith cards per day.

H. J. McDonald, the IBM salesman who sold and handled the SSA account, recalled that Thomas J. Watson ordered the development of a special collator, the IBM 077, because "the Social Security agency punched cards from records sent in by employers all over the country. There were millions and millions of them, and if we hadn't had some way of putting them all together we would have been lost; we just couldn't have done it." The IBM mechanical machines were so reliable, accurate, and successful that they were used for years. Government checks are still issued as special Hollerith punch cards. In addition, these tabulating and sorting machines gave the federal government the capability to establish national programs to handle individual citizens. The IBM machines made it possible, for example, to institute the withholding tax in 1943.

However, the ability of the mechanical computers to crunch numbers, albeit slowly by modern standards, led people to push them to their limits. The mechanical computers also convinced people that there were other problems that could be solved if computers were faster and larger. But the mechanical computers were indeed limited. A new type of computer had to be discovered.

Looking back on it, it's possible to see that all the elements were there to develop the electronic computer—the computer that used low-mass electrons moving at or near the speed of light instead of heavy mechanical linkages. Dr. Lee De Forest's audio triode vacuum tube had been perfected and improved; it was in wide use in radio and telephone communications. But one element was missing: a theoretical foundation for the operation of electronic digital computers.

Two men arrived at the same solution almost simultaneously, but from different directions and for different reasons.

In 1937, Claude E. Shannon wrote his master's thesis at MIT describing a way to improve telephone switching circuits using the symbolic logic of George Boole. Shannon didn't invent "binary notation," which is the way to count using only two numbers, zero and one. But he did show how to use it. In one example entitled "Electric Adder to the Base Two," he designed the electrical circuitry. His thesis was published in *Transactions of the American Institute of Electrical Engineers.* It provided the theoretical basis for the entire set of programming operations that would later be designed into electronic digital computers. Shannon's thesis proved something that others later discovered, forcing them to come back to his thesis for solutions: the biggest programming problem in digital computers didn't lie in arithmetic, but in logic.

In the same year, George Stibitz independently built such an adder on his kitchen table from "some relays from a scrap heap at Bell Labs where I then worked." He named it after the kitchen table: Model K. Stibitz solved the problems empirically, building relay calculators of increasing complexity during the next ten years. He didn't know anything about Shannon's work, so he worked out the principles of binary notation and machine logic as he went along.

Everything was then in place for the next great breakthrough in the computer revolution: the electron takeover. However, the mechanical computer had one last hurrah.

In 1937, Howard H. Aiken, then a graduate student at Harvard, proposed the development of a new kind of calculating machine because "there exist problems beyond our ability to solve, not because of theoretical difficulties, but because of insufficient means of mechanical computation." Aiken knew they'd reached the end of the rope for simple mechanical adding machines, although his first proposal suggested linking together a bank of Monroe mechanical desk calculators in a "player piano" principle to create a large scientific calculator with several "registers" in which to store numbers as they were being worked on.

In his 1937 proposal, Aiken pointed out some of the technical fields that needed more computer power if scientists and engineers were not to spend their days in a continuous battle with complex mathematics, physics of the upper atmosphere, astronomy, relativity, and the "science of mathematical economy."

But no one at Harvard had the technical expertise to assist Aiken. So astronomer Harlow Shapley sent him to see the people at IBM.

Thomas J. Watson, always on the lookout for new ways to use computers and new concepts in computer design, was impressed with Aiken and his ideas. In 1938, he assigned IBM engineers Clair D. Lake, Francis E. Hamilton, and Benjamin M. Durfee to work with Aiken on the development of a large general-purpose digital calculator that came to be known as the "Automatic Sequence Controlled Calculator." At Harvard, it was always known as simply the "Mark 1." It took them six years to develop this strange hybrid computer, which still used mechanical components such as relays and mechanical input-output devices. But it was programmable and digital, the first of its kind.

The Mark 1 was a clicking, chattering monster when it was finally turned on in the IBM plant in Endicott, New York, in 1943. It weighed five tons and contained thirty-three hundred electromechanical relays. Rolls of punched card stock, punched cards, paper tape, or manually set rotary switches were used for inputs. The Mark 1 had four tape readers. Three of these were used for read-only memory or "interpolation," and the fourth was the sequence control. As engineer L. J. Comrie explained: "The brains of the machine lie in the control tape, which is code-punched in three sections. The first instructs the machine where to find its data; the second gives the destination of the data or answer; the third dictates the process." Some tapes held instructions or the program for the problem being run. Others held standard subroutines, which could be stored and then used when the master program required them.

The ASCC or "Mark 1" was delivered to Harvard in February 1944 and was up and on line by April. Its first task was to compute ballistic tables for the U.S. Navy. It was also used in naval ship design, lens design, and number crunching for Wright Patterson Air Force Base and, eventually, the U.S. Atomic Energy Commission. The Mark 1 became the foundation for the Harvard Computation Laboratory, where Aiken encouraged people to use it and subsequent electronic computers to solve their computational problems in such fields as economics, insurance, physics, and linguistics. The Harvard Mark 1's electromechanical relays kept right on chittering and chattering until it was scrapped in 1959.

But it epitomized the computer because it was obsolete at

the moment the IBM engineers first switched it on in Endicott in 1943. The vacuum tube was taking over, making computers totally electronic.

This was accelerated by the demands of wartime on technology. The concept of automation was now more firmly rooted in the minds of many people. Although the conduct of armed conflict requires the exercise of human judgment, there were many military activities that could be assumed by automatic machinery. Computers had been used to calculate exterior ballistics, the flight of artillery shells from gun to target. This had been carried out in a calculating laboratory; men still had to apply the results from the ballistics tables under pressure in the field. Now, if computers and automata could be made portable so that they could serve in self-regulating, feedback-controlled systems in the field . . .

This actually came about as a result of one of those wartime dreams that plague even men who haven't been in combat. Shortly after the evacuation of the British Expeditionary Force from Dunkirk in 1940, Bell Telephone Laboratories engineer David B. Parkinson had such a dream. He dreamt he was with a Dutch antiaircraft battery, which had a wonderful robot that tracked the incoming German Stukas, computed the information, predicted where the airplanes would be, then directed the aiming and firing of the antiaircraft guns with incredible accuracy.

When Parkinson woke up, his dream sounded feasible. He got Bell Labs interested, and they got the U.S. Army Ordnance Corps excited. With his Bell Labs colleagues, Clarence A. Lovell and Bruce T. Weber, Parkinson developed his dream to reality. It was called the M-9 Gun Director.

The M-9 was one of the first goal-seeking machines. After radar locked onto a target, it regulated itself. It used an internal program that included the ballistic data on the 90-millimeter antiaircraft gun. It calculated the course of the incoming airplane, compared that against the outgoing trajectory of the 90-millimeter shell, told the gun where to point, and ordered the firing of the shell so that airplane and shell met at the same time in the same place. To do this, it used automatic calculation and feedback control of the sort originally developed by Elmer and Lawrence Sperry for aircraft gyro autopilots in 1914. However,

Parkinson and his colleagues at Bell Labs now had the vacuum tube, which had been used for almost a decade in telephone amplifier circuits. The unique part of the M-9 was its "operational amplifier," which used vacuum tubes to control electrical voltages that were analogs to mechanical variables. It was as fast as the electrons coursing through the vacuums in its tubes and down its wires. Its output voltages drove electrical servomotors that turned the guns in azimuth and elevation.

The M-9 really worked, and the Axis powers had nothing like it. In the Allied air defense of Antwerp in October 1944, 90-millimeter antiaircraft guns directed by M-9s engaged 4,883 German V-1 "buzz bombs" and shot down 4,617 of them—an amazing accuracy of 95.7 percent, totally unheard of in the annals of antiaircraft artillery. On the last day of the attack, 89 of the 91 attacking German V-1s were destroyed. The German V-1 (Feisler FZG 76) itself was an unmanned robot-guided, bomb-carrying airplane using gyroscopic control and an aerodynamically actuated mechanical dive initiator; once launched, the V-1 would fly straight and level until a mechanical counter had totaled up a predetermined number of revolutions of a small propeller on the nose, which, when the total was achieved, programmed the V-1 into a dive. Here was the first robot war.

The M-9's operational amplifier made the electronic analog computer possible and totally replaced the mechanical machines such as the Bush differential analyzer. It also became the foundation upon which electronic digital computers were then built.

The two basic types of computers could be differentiated by the early 1940s: the analog and the digital computer. These two different computers can be easily understood by considering their earliest examples: the slide rule and the abacus.

A slide rule—if you can find one these days—is an analog computer. It uses lengths as analogs for quantities. If a length of one inch is equal to the number 1, two inches for 2, and so forth, it's possible to add numbers by adding dimensions. Thus, if you add a 12-inch stick to a 15-inch stick, you will have a total length of 27 inches. Worked out by arithmetic, that's 12 + 15 = 27. A "linear" scale has been used in this example. But it's possible to do multiplication and division on a slide rule if the analog distance scales are set up on a logarithmic basis because when two logarithms are added together, the antilogarithm of the result is the same as multiplying the two original numbers together.

There are problems with analog computers. In the case of the slide rule, it's a matter of placing the decimal point because the "slip-stick" doesn't tell you where the decimal point is. As a result, scientists, mathematicians, and engineers had to learn how to interpolate the results to locate it. This encouraged the user to get a feel for the "ball park numbers" involved with the problem. One anticipated that the results of 100.25 times 4.67 would be somewhere about 400—actually 481.16 plus a little something—rather than somewhere around 40 or 4000. In working with digital pocket calculators with floating point programs, one doesn't worry about decimal points and therefore tends to take the computer's results in full faith without bothering to question a number that would seem, to a person who cut his technical teeth on a slide rule, out of the ball park.

Analog computers are only as accurate as it is possible to measure their analog quantities. In the case of the slide rule, it was considered acceptable to get between three- and four-digit accuracies from a twelve-inch slip stick. Six-inch slide rules, although more portable, are smaller and therefore less accurate; they were primarily used for quick-look calculations. Few engineers had access to twenty-four-inch slide rules. In order to increase the length and therefore the accuracy of slide rules, some designs were circular and others had their scales wrapped as spirals down long tubes.

On the other hand, the digital computer works with discrete numbers. In the case of the basic digital computer, the Oriental abacus, numbers are represented by beads on wires. Move a bead from bottom to top or top to bottom, and you've either entered an integral number or subtracted same. You can't work with half a number, only a whole number. If you want half a number, you've got to add other beads on an adjacent wire, put an imaginary decimal point between the two wires, then work in decimal values of the whole number, not in fractions.

A digital computer is fast. In a big city, visit Chinatown and watch a merchant total a sale on an abacus with amazing speed.

A digital computer is as accurate as the number of integers it is capable of handling. An abacus with nine rows of counters is accurate to nine digits, just as a pocket computer with an eight-digit capacity is accurate to eight digits. An abacus will not round off the last digit; the operator must do that mentally if necessary; a pocket calculator usually has rounding off built into its program.

A digital computer is accurate unless it drops a digit somewhere in the computing process.

In most cases, either an analog or a digital computer is accurate enough for most daily use. Five-digit accuracy is enough to enable most of us to run our everyday lives, although some people are able to use the full eight-digit capability of a modern digital computer when it comes to balancing their checkbooks.

To put it in its simplest terms: an analog computer measures beans laid end to end. A digital computer counts beans one at a time.

The analog computer's biggest requirement is increased accuracy to measure the beans. The digital computer needs increased speed to count the beans.

And the latter was the big reason why Aiken's Mark 1 became almost instantly obsolete.

With the outbreak of World War II in 1939, the U.S. Army Ordnance Corps set out to improve the differential analyzers and other computational means used at its Aberdeen Proving Ground for calculating ballistic tables. In spite of the work done there in World War I, many variables hadn't been properly accounted for. In the first place, there was little data regarding some of them. Some factors affecting the flight of shells, such as atmospheric drag, weren't defined by mathematical formulas; they were "empirical" numbers derived from actual tests and other measurements. To do such calculations, Aberdeen employed two hundred women who did nothing eight hours a day but punch numbers into mechanical calculators such as those built by Burroughs, Monroe, Friden, and Marchant. Using this slow method, a ballistic table could be completed for one type of gun under a given set of conditions in a time of two to three months. Even when the existing mechanical differential analyzers had been upgraded and improved to their absolute limits, their accuracies and speeds could be increased only by a factor of ten—still far too inaccurate and slow for the work that needed to be done. By 1944, when the United States was fully involved in the war, requests for completely new ballistics tables were flooding into Aberdeen at the rate of six per day. Each of these demanded the calculation of hundreds of trajectories. A skilled person with a desk calculator could compute a single sixty-second trajectory in twenty hours. The differential analyzers produced the same result in fifteen minutes, provided the numbers for the various empirical factors had been hand-computed beforehand.

Three men came up with the answer, as well as the first general-purpose electronic digital computer.

J. Presper Eckert built his first radio at the age of five. He earned a degree in electrical engineering from the University of Pennsylvania in 1941 and became a graduate fellow at the university's Moore School of Electrical Engineering.

John W. Mauchly started out as an engineering student at Johns Hopkins University, but switched to physics and earned his Ph.D. in 1934. He took a position teaching physics at Ursinus College near Philadelphia, where, in 1941, he met Eckert.

The third member of the triumvirate was Captain Herman H. Goldstine, U.S. Army Ordnance Corps, stationed at Aberdeen Proving Ground, who later said that his role in the development of the first electronic digital computer was nothing more than "being in the right place at the right time."

There was considerable communication between the War Department and the academic world prior to World War II, primarily as a result of early contacts made during the previous "war to end all wars." Eckert and Mauchly, both in the Philadelphia area, knew each other and learned of the Army's computational problems at Aberdeen, which is practically "just down the road" from Philadelphia and readily accessible via one of the few fast railways in America. They determined that the Aberdeen computational problem could be solved by a digital calculator that would do the jobs of both the differential analyzer and the human calculators.

On April 2, 1943, they submitted a memo to Aberdeen describing an "ELECTRONIC DIFF* ANALYZER" that would produce a complete ballistic table in less than two days. To do this, they would utilize vacuum tubes rather than electromechanical relays as on-off switches because the switching time of a vacuum tube was faster by orders of magnitude. Under contract to the U.S. Army Ordnance Corps, with Captain Goldstine as project officer, Eckert and Mauchly began planning their machine in 1943.

They called it the "ENIAC," an acronym for Electronic Numerical Integrator And Computer.

Although the operating elements of ENIAC were submicroscopic electrons, ENIAC itself was huge and hot because the electronic components of that time were huge. When ENIAC was formally dedicated at the Moore School of Electrical Engineering in February 1946, almost a year after World War II ended, it covered fifteen hundred square feet of floor space on the first floor of the Moore School. It weighed thirty tons. It contained more than thirty thousand vacuum tubes assembled in plug-in modules, each capable of handling a "decade" of numbers and containing twenty-eight vacuum tubes with their assorted wiring, capacitors, resistors, coils, transformers, and connectors. ENIAC's central processor had two hundred such decade units, giving the computer a total working memory capacity of twenty ten-digit numbers. It was capable of performing three hundred multiplications per second, in contrast to the best electromechanical computers, which could do one per second.

But ENIAC had to be rewired for each new program. This involved manually resetting switches and reconnecting cables. It took a long time and a lot of effort to reprogram ENIAC. But once it started number crunching, it was the fastest thing on earth. The ENIAC's main job was to be "faster than a speeding bullet" and complete the calculations of a projectile's flight in less time than it took for the projectile itself to cover the trajectory. This it could do, computing a trajectory in half the time it took the projectile to do it. Although the war was over ENIAC was used for the lengthy and repetitive calculations involved in generating ballistic tables. It was also put to use on a wide variety of scientific and technical problems such as early attempts at computerization of meteorological data for weather prediction, nuclear energy calculations, cosmic ray studies, thermal ignition, random-number generation, and aerodynamic wind-tunnel design.

ENIAC kept right on crunching numbers until 1950, long past the time when it had been rendered obsolete by its progeny.

The Harvard Mark 1 and ENIAC, the first large general-purpose digital computers, required someone to tell them what to do. The profession of programmer was born. The first programmers were mathematicians. But the manpower demands of World War II left few male mathematicians available. As in many other established fields, women stepped in and took over. Most of the early computer programmers were women not only for this reason, but also because, being a totally new profession, there were no established precedents, and the computers didn't care.

Actually, programming also began in the 1820s concurrent with Charles Babbage's development of his analytical engine. Lord Byron's daughter, Ada Augusta, the Countess of Lovelace, was a skilled mathematician and a close friend of Babbage. In a detailed mathematical analysis of the Babbage machine, she developed many of the basic concepts of programming just as Babbage himself laid the basic foundations for computers.

But it was during the development of ENIAC that Adele Goldstine, Captain Herman Goldstine's mathematician wife, became the first programmer for ENIAC. There were no high-level languages then. Not even the concept of machine language yet. Adele Goldstine had to work out in advance the exact interconnection of all the elements of ENIAC.

Not all those called to the colors during World War II were men. Mathematician Dr. Grace Hopper was an officer in the Naval Reserve. She began her long and productive career as a programmer for Aiken's Harvard Mark 1.

Just as the card punch, tabulator, and sorter in concert with the typewriter opened the office world to women, the general-purpose digital computer continued to provide the drive for the liberation of not only men but women. And it continues today.

By 1946, the electrons had taken over, and the Norbert Weiner's goal of the human use of human beings—men *and* women together—was just beginning.

10

The Vacuum Tube Monsters

The ENIAC of Eckert and Mauchly was unquestionably a breakthrough, although other companies such as IBM, Burroughs, and NCR report that they also had electronic computers under development in their labs circa 1940, but that the exigencies of war precluded them from proceeding rapidly with these developments.

And there's no question that, effective and advanced as it was at the time, ENIAC had problems. Not the least among these was the difficulty in programming it. Again, happenstance opened a new path toward future developments and progress.

On one of Captain Herman H. Goldstine's many train trips between Aberdeen and Philadelphia during the development of ENIAC at the Moore School, he had a chance encounter at the Aberdeen railroad station with Dr. John von Neumann of Princeton's Institute for Advanced Study. At the time, von Neumann was involved with the Army Engineers' Manhattan District, builders of the atomic bomb, and was on one of his many train trips between Princeton and Aberdeen. As they waited for the train to come, they engaged in casual conversation. Goldstine spoke of the unclassified ENIAC program, its potential, and its problems. Von Neumann became intrigued.

For over a hundred years, and especially during the preceding fifty, the three lines of development of calculating machines, statistical machines, and logical automata had been converging.

The principles and techniques developed for gun directors, calculators, and punch-card accounting machines were rapidly being combined. ENIAC was but one consequence. The modern computer needed a single additional concept in order to achieve the final fusion of these three areas.

The people working hard on the development and programming of the Mark 1 and the ENIAC missed it, although they were right in the middle of it. John von Neumann saw it immediately and intuitively.

John von Neumann was born in Hungary and received his early education in Europe before World War II. He studied chemistry and mathematics at the universities of Budapest and Berlin and at the Technische Hochschule in Zurich. When he was twenty-four, he was appointed a *privatdozent* at the University of Berlin. A *privatdozent* is the highest of all possible academic ranks. The individual is neither tenured nor salaried; rather, he is paid directly by his students. Von Neumann came to Princeton University in 1930 as a lecturer in mathematical physics. In 1933, he became a permanent member of the Institute for Advanced Study there. He was well liked by everyone and was known as a brilliant and hard-working man "who could talk faster in any of seven languages than most people can in their own."

The enormously complex mathematical problems inherent in designing and building the first atomic bombs in the Manhattan District (named the "Manhattan Project" by the press) gave von Neumann an appreciation for the value of large, fast, accurate computing machines.

John von Neumann looked over Goldstine's ENIAC. When the Army asked for bids on a more advanced and more powerful calculator than the ENIAC, von Neumann responded with a report in which he developed the complete logical design of a machine he called EDVAC (Electronic Discrete Variable Automatic Computer). He had worked with Adele Goldstine on the development of a wiring scheme for ENIAC that allowed it to interpret other programs and act upon them in the same manner as if the programs had originally been wired into or stored in the ENIAC. Therefore, his EDVAC proposal contained a totally new concept based on his work with Adele Goldstine on ENIAC. He suggested that computer instructions, which had always been entered on punched tape or with plugboards, could be stored in the computer's electronic memory as numbers and treated as ordinary numerical data. This would allow logical choices of programs to be made *inside* the machine, and instructions to alter this internal program could be modified by the computer or put in from outside as the program proceeded.

Every modern computer uses von Neumann's "stored program" concept. Few people realized it was developed as a result of a chance conversation on a rural Maryland station platform while waiting for a train that was, in wartime, always late.

Von Neumann didn't stop there. He wanted an ENIAC-type computer of his own that he could play with, alter, change, and develop. But the Institute of Advanced Studies (IAS) had a firm policy of doing absolutely no experimental work; it was strictly a high-powered scientific think tank that left the hardware to others. But John von Neumann's influence (and persuasiveness) was so strong that the IAS made an exception in his case so that he and his group could construct a fully automatic, digital, all-purpose computing machine. In his justification, von Neumann wrote: "It is to be expected that the future evolution of high-speed computing will be decisively influenced by the experiences gained."

The war over, von Neumann brought Goldstine into his group at IAS, where Arthur Burkes joined with ENIAC builders Eckert and Mauchly to produce an elaborate "detailed outline" for the IAS computer (which was never named in the acronymic style of the other computers of the late 1940s).

The IAS computer also incorporated the principle of internal electrostatic storage in what von Neumann, Goldstine, and Burks called the "Selectron" tube, a device that could store 4,096 binary digits. Today, the Selectron would be called an electrostatic 4K RAM. The first IAS model used 40 Selectrons to get a memory of 160K.

The ENIAC triggered the development of many similar computers other than EDVAC and the IAS computer. There were perhaps fifteen different types in all. Among them were:

ENIAC: Electronic Numerical Integrator And Computer

EDVAC: Electronic Discrete Variable Automatic Computer

   EDSAC: Electronic Delay Storage Automatic Compu-
ter
   MADM: Manchester Automatic Digital Machine
   SEAC: Standards Eastern Automatic Computer
   SWAC: Standards Western Automatic Computer
   MANIAC: Mathematical Analyzer, Numerical Integra-
tor, And Computer

All of them were electronic digital stored-program machines, but the technologies used in each differed greatly. This
was because von Neumann's report on the design of the EDVAC
allowed a wide variety of technological solutions. This was
advantageous to progress in the field because it permitted the
early computer engineers to learn what worked best.

While this early electronic general computer development
was going on, IBM wasn't content just to sit in the wings with
its electromechanical punch-card machines. The company
came out from under wartime activities and restrictions to
plunge headlong into the electronic computer race. In the
commercial field, to take up the slack between the old prewar
mechanical calculators and the new electronic computers, IBM
produced the first small commercial electronic calculator, the
IBM 603 Multiplier in 1946. One hundred were delivered,
starting in 1946. This was followed by the IBM 604, the first
calculator to supplant electromechanical business equipment.
Like the ENIAC, it used replaceable modules of electronic
components—vacuum tubes plus related capacitors and resistors—on single chassis units that could be removed or installed
without tools.

Independently of von Neumann, IBM developed the stored
program concept and incorporated it into the IBM Selective
Sequence Electronic Calculator, or SSEC. When it became
operational on January 28, 1948, it was the first machine
capable of storing and operating on its instructions as if they
were data. The SSEC was installed where the world could see it,
behind huge plate-glass windows on the street floor of IBM's
World Headquarters, then at Fifty-seventh Street and Madison
Avenue in New York City. The inscription on SSEC by Thomas
J. Watson prophesied: "This machine will assist the scientist in
institutions of learning, in government, and in industry to

explore the consequences of man's thought to the outmost reaches of time, space, and physical conditions." Known as the "Oracle on Fifty-seventh Street," SSEC was a strange hybrid. It contained 12,500 vacuum tubes and 21,400 electromechanical relays. It used punched paper tape for memory storage. It could add or subtract nineteen-digit numbers in less than three hundred microseconds, making it more than one hundred times faster than the purely electromechanical Harvard Mark 1 of less than five years before. The SSEC operated for four years and helped solve problems in fluid flow, planetary orbits, optics, hydrodynamics, and other scientific and technical areas that could not be effectively addressed in any other manner.

Then, as now, computers had their doubters and scoffers, especially among some scientists and mathematicians who were afraid that their professions were doomed by these new superfast adding machines. One mathematician flatly stated that the SSEC would never amount to much for the following reasons:

1. The average life of a vacuum tube was three thousand hours.
2. The SSEC had more than twelve thousand vacuum tubes.
3. Based on the laws of probability, a tube failure would occur every fifteen minutes.
4. It would take more than fifteen minutes to find the bad tube.
5. Therefore, the SSEC would never be able to do any useful work.

It didn't happen, of course, primarily because a lot of work went into quality control. Premium pretested vacuum tubes were selected for installation in the SSEC, and IBM engineers worked out failure-reporting techniques that would allow a technician to replace a bad module in minutes. In fact, most of the flashing lights associated with today's Hollywood movie computers derive from the SSEC's control panels where the lights were merely indicators that everything was working properly.

A thorough and careful marketing study was made in 1949 and it found that there was no real market for computers because nine SSECs would be adequate to handle all the data-processing and scientific computing tasks of the entire United States for decades to come.

Eckert and Mauchly decided there might be a future in the computer industry, in spite of the poor market forecast, so they left the University of Pennsylvania and formed their own firm, the Electronic Control Company, with headquarters at 1215 Walnut Street in Philadelphia. Another move put them at Broad and Spring Garden streets, and they changed the firm name to the Eckert-Mauchly Computer Corporation. In 1949, they completed a test vehicle computer called BINAC (Binary Automatic Computer) at yet another location, Ridge Avenue in North Philadelphia.

The word *binary* refers to the basic numbering system used by all computers. Human beings work in a decimal system "to the base ten" probably because we have ten fingers, which were our first counting units. In the binary system only two numbers are required, zero and one. The reason a computer uses the binary system is that the two numbers, zero and one, can be represented by two states: *off* and *on*. A computer can recognize the hole or lack of a hole in a punch card, for example. It can recognize the presence or absence of an electrical pulse. It can respond to an open or a closed switch, or a vacuum tube or other electronic component that acts like a switch and is either in a condition to conduct an electrical signal or not to conduct it. It can interpret magnetic spots on disks or tapes as "zero" or "one." Various coding systems are therefore used to translate letters of the alphabet and decimal numbers into the zeroes and ones of computer language.

In the basic binary code, each digit doubles in value from right to left. For example, the number 9 is represented in a string of pulses by the "on" condition that has a value of 1 and the "on" condition in the place that has a value of 8:

Binary Code:	0	0	0	0	1	0	0	1
Binary value:	128	64	32	16	8	4	2	1

Each binary number in the code is called a "bit." A string of eight binary numbers is called an "8-bit" word, or a "byte."

Today, a national binary code for numbers and letters of the alphabet has been standardized. Called the "ASCII Code," it is shown here only partially:

Decimal Number	Binary Number
	8 4 2 1
0	0 0 0 0
1	0 0 0 1
2	0 0 1 0
3	0 0 1 1
4	0 1 0 0
5	0 1 0 1
6	0 1 1 0
7	0 1 1 1
8	1 0 0 0
9	1 0 0 1

Letter	Binary Number
A	1 1 0 0 0 1
B	1 1 0 0 1 0
C	1 1 0 0 1 1
D	1 1 0 1 0 0
E	1 1 0 1 0 1
F	1 1 0 1 1 0
G	1 1 0 1 1 1
H	1 1 1 0 0 0
I	1 1 1 0 0 1
J	1 1 1 0 1 0
K	1 1 1 0 1 1

Other written symbols such as commas, periods, and question marks have been assigned their own discrete binary number.

But when Eckert and Mauchly built the BINAC, this coding hadn't been standardized. They had to work it out themselves from scratch.

BINAC was the test machine that led the two men directly to the world's first well-known digital computer, which they also started in 1949 and called the Universal Automatic Computer, or UNIVAC.

UNIVAC was a general-purpose alpha-numeric machine

that could handle both numbers and letters. It could use nearly all the input-output devices—"peripherals"—of the time such as punch-card readers, magnetic tape, and teletype printers. It was also able to simultaneously read, compute, and record data. It used a mercury delay line memory in which binary data was recycled through the liquid metal in the form of acoustical pulses that were read and automatically reintroduced into the delay line at the beginning. This process could go on indefinitely so that the data could be stored. In 1949, ten thousand *tons* of punch cards were being used in the United States every year, and Eckert and Mauchly therefore developed a new method of storing large quantities of data in a small amount of space. UNIVAC 1 introduced magnetic tape as a storage medium, but the tape was iron-plated metal rather than plastic with iron-oxide coating, as it is today. Data from the UNIVAC's memory could be processed in about 0.2 seconds or 200 milliseconds (thousandths of a second).

Before UNIVAC 1 was completed, the Eckert-Mauchly Computer Corporation was acquired by Remington Rand, Inc., in 1950.

Following in the steps of Herman Hollerith sixty years later, the first UNIVAC 1 was delivered to the U.S. Bureau of the Census on June 14, 1951, and was put to work on the 1950 United States Census.

UNIVAC 1 had only about five thousand vacuum tubes—not as many as the IBM SSEC—but weighed sixteen thousand pounds. It was, however, an *electronic* computer without electromechanical relays in its operating system, a unique animal at the time.

And UNIVAC 1 was *fast* for its time, capable of performing a single operation in about a millisecond.

UNIVAC 1 became a television celebrity, when CBS News used it to predict the outcome of the 1952 presidential elections, the first time a computer was used for this purpose. Long before the polls closed in all states, the results from early returns were entered into UNIVAC 1. The computer then predicted, on the basis of past election results from key precincts—information that had previously been entered into its memory—that Dwight D. Eisenhower would defeat Adlai E. Stevenson by 438 electoral votes to 93. UNIVAC 1's forecast was very close. The actual count came out 442 to 89.

The electronic digital computer was suddenly perceived as a super, omniscient electrical brain. As the years went by and more sophisticated election prediction programs and better precinct data became available, along with faster and bigger computers, the business of accurately predicting an election's outcome on the basis of a small percentage of critical precinct results actually began to affect elections themselves. Critics claim that early computer election predictions discourage late voters from going to the polls, thereby having a strong impact on the overall election process. We have yet to see the end of the trend that UNIVAC 1 started in 1952.

UNIVAC 1 was a giant. But to make the next step forward, Remington Rand acquired Engineering Research Associates (ERA) of St. Paul, Minnesota, in 1952. ERA was a group of mathematicians and engineers who had been active in the development of computerlike electronic cryptographic equipment during World War II. Cryptography involves making and breaking codes and ciphers, a job now universally accepted as being something tailor-made for computers. ERA's work in this field led them into data processing after World War II and resulted in the delivery of some fast scientific computers to the United States Navy and Georgia Institute of Technology in 1950. When Remington Rand acquired them, they combined the ERA technology with their own UNIVAC know-how, giving birth to the UNIVAC 1101.

In contrast to UNIVAC 1's limited mercury delay line storage and iron-coated magnetic tape memory systems, the UNIVAC 1101 used rotating magnetic drums as memory storage units, pioneering the various magnetic storage peripherals such as the hard disks, tape drives, and floppy disks of today.

UNIVAC 1101 was probably the first computer to go on-line to provide real-time data. It was connected to the analog sensors in the wind tunnel at Wright-Patterson Air Force Base in Dayton, Ohio. The analog sensor output was digitized, transmitted to the UNIVAC 1101, computer processed, converted back to analog form, and fed back to the wind tunnel to help control and adjust its performance within very tight limits. The first commercial unit, the UNIVAC 1103, was delivered in 1953. An improved version of the 1101, using magnetic-core storage instead of rotating drums, was two thousand times faster than its immediate predecessor because the core memory could be accessed electronically rather than mechanically.

The final link between the computing machine, the statistical machine, and the logical automata was completed when in 1955 Remington Rand, Inc., and the Sperry Corporation were consolidated into the Sperry Rand Corporation.

By 1954, vacuum tube computers were becoming more numerous, powerful, and faster. IBM's Naval Ordnance Research Computer (NORC) had more than nine thousand vacuum tubes and could multiply two thirteen-digit numbers in thirty-one millionths of a second (microseconds), including properly placing the decimal point. (To gain some perspective on technological progress, today's $9.95 pocket calculator, weighing about an ounce, can multiply two eight-digit numbers and properly place the decimal point in about a microsecond.)

The largest of all vacuum tube computers was SAGE (Semi-Automatic Ground Environment), built by IBM for the United States Air Force as part of the U.S. air defense system in the 1950s. Twenty-seven SAGE computers were installed. Each had 58,000 vacuum tubes, weighed 113 tons, and consumed enough power to supply a town of 15,000 people. It provided "real-time" man-machine interaction in the radar air defense system. Information on flying aircraft was fed into SAGE from hundreds of radar sites linked by 1.5 million miles of communications links from all over the North American continent. SAGE was the precursor to the modern air traffic control system, and some SAGE computers remained in service as part of that system until as late as 1983.

But the days of the vacuum tube computer were already numbered. They were big. They required kilowatts of power, most of which went to heat up the tiny tungsten filaments inside the vacuum tubes. Most of this energy was wasted as heat, which in turn meant that these vacuum tube monsters required enormous amounts of refrigerated air conditioning.

The device that replaced the vacuum tube came from what might be considered an unlikely place.

George Stibitz, the man who built one of the first electromechanical relay calculators on his kitchen table, the Model K, had left Bell Labs in 1941 to spend the war years as a technical aid to the National Defense Research Council. Returning to Bell

Labs, Stibitz built the closest thing to Charles Babbage's analytical engine, the great steam-powered assembly of brass gears, cams, and wheels that was never built. Stibitz's Model V relay computer was completed in 1946. It incorporated all Babbage's concepts. Information was entered into the Stibitz machines (he built five different models for Bell Labs) via three standard teletype machines. This caused problems, Stibitz recalled: "There was a certain amount of sneaky behavior on the part of operators trying to get to a teletype and turn it on before the other teletypes could be occupied because what we had then for time-sharing did not allow two people to work at the same time."

The Stibitz computers built at Bell Labs used a common telephone component, the electromechanical relay. Bell Labs people became good designers of relay-type equipment, including computers. But some of Bell's long-distance equipment used vacuum tubes as analog amplifiers of voice signals. The problems involved with using vacuum tubes in remote telephone line amplifiers buried underground or in overseas cables resembled similar problems in computers: vacuum tubes required lots of power, had limited lifetimes, and produced wasted heat from their filaments. There had to be a better way to do the job. It was Bell Labs' job to find such a solution.

John H. Patterson bought the first cash register ever made, and he liked it so much he bought the company, too. He founded the National Cash Register Company (now NCR Corporation) and served as its president until 1921. He originated the famous "THINK!" signs in the workplace. *(NCR photo)*

William S. Burroughs, inventor and co-founder of the American Arithmometer Company, later to become the Burroughs Corporation. *(Photo courtesy Burroughs Corporation)*

The first wood-cased cash register designed and sold by National Cash Register Company and one of the first computers. *(NCR Photo)*

An early-1900 model Burroughs "Style No. 3" adding and listing machine with glass sides exposing the inner workings (a gimmick used to promote sales). *(Photo courtesy Burroughs Corporation)*

The Hollerith Pantograph Punch was first used in the 1890 U.S. Census. Able to punch forty columns of round holes in the Hollerith punch card, it was the predecessor of more complex card punching machinery. *(Courtesy IBM Corporation archives)*

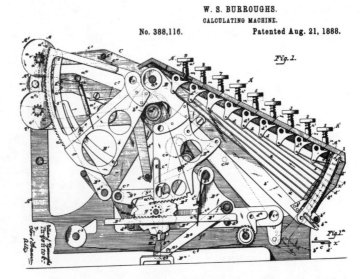

W. S. BURROUGHS.
CALCULATING MACHINE.
No. 388,116.   Patented Aug. 21, 1888.

Fig.1.

The patent drawing of the Burroughs mechanical adding machine, which received the first patent ever issued for a computer. *(Photo courtesy Burroughs Corporation)*

Thomas J. Watson, Sr., founder of IBM. *(Courtesy IBM Corporation)*

Dr. Herman Hollerith. *(Courtesy IBM Corporation archives)*

David Packard *(left)* and Bill Hewlett, founders of Hewlett-Packard, one of the first Silicon Valley electronic companies *(Hewlett-Packard photo)*

Computer-age entrepreneurs Carole Ely *(left)* and Lore Harp formed Vector Graphic, Inc., in a suburban California home and built it into a multimillion-dollar business and personal computer company in less than eight years. *(Vector Graphic, Inc. photo)*

One of the original Hollerith card punch machines (on desk), the Hollerith punch card tabulator with its forty summation dial counters, and the Hollerith sorter box (at right). This first practical data management machine was developed for and used by the U.S. Census by Dr. Herman Hollerith. *(Courtesy IBM Corporation archives)*

The UNIVAC/ERA 1103 was widely used for scientific and technical work, especially in the field of rocketry and guided missiles. This ERA 1103 was installed at White Sands, New Mexico, in 1955. *(U.S. Army photo)*

ENIAC, the world's first electronic digital computer, was assembled at the University of Pennsylvania's Moore School of Electrical Engineering and was completed in 1946. It used 18,000 vacuum tubes and weighed 130 tons. *(Sperry Corporation photo)*

The IBM Selective Sequence Electronic Calculator, one of the first vacuum-tube computers to come out of World War II. *(Courtesy IBM Corporation)*

The UNIVAC 1 was used by CBS to forecast the outcome of the 1952 presidential election. Here newsman Walter Cronkite and UNIVAC 1 builder Dr. J. Presper Eckert review preliminary results. *(Sperry Corporation photo)*

The Burroughs UDEC (United Digital Electronic Computer) was typical of the computer of the late 1950s. It had three thousand vacuum tubes, seven thousand transistors, and ten miles of wire. *(Photo courtesy Burroughs Corporation)*

The IBM Automatic Sequence Controlled Calculator with its banks of relays and vacuum tubes. *(Courtesy IBM Corporation)*

The Hewlett-Packard HP-35 of 1972 was a hand-held scientific calculator that made the slide rule obsolete. *(Hewlett-Packard photo)*

The miniscule modern 64 kilobyte memory chip fabricated with large-scale integrated (LSI) circuit technology. *(Courtesy IBM Corporation)*

This is a closeup of the twenty-three thousand microscopic circuits of the Intel Corporation 4004 microprocessor chip, the first of its kind. It's simple compared to a 1984 model microprocessor, which may have more than one hundred thousand circuits. *(Intel Corp. photo)*

The Burroughs E101 desk-size computer of the 1950s used a magnetic drum memory and was programmed for scientific, engineering, and business applications by using pins in a plug board. *(Photo courtesy Burroughs Corporation)*

A typical small business computer, the Vector Graphic MZ/3032, with a combined keypad and CRT screen and the main frame incorporated into an enclosure along with minifloppy diskette drives *(Vector Graphic, Inc. photo)*

The typical modern personal computer. This is the IBM PC personal computer that shook the microcomputer industry when it appeared in 1981. *(Courtesy IBM Corporation)*

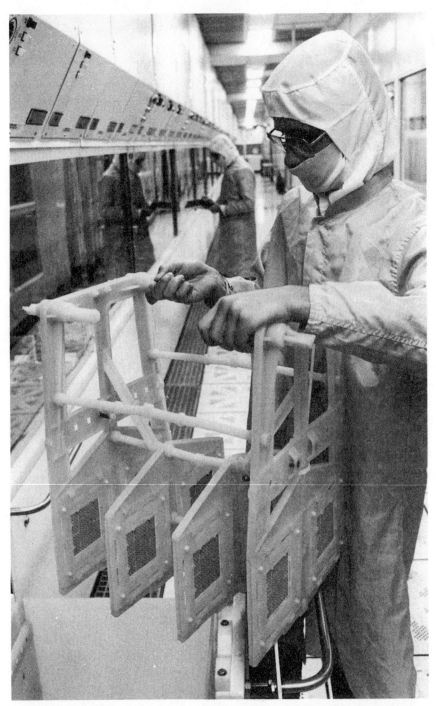

Extreme cleanliness is essential in the manufacture of integrated circuit chips. The air must be two thousand times more pure than that in a hospital operating room. Personnel wear special clothing to eliminate lint and other contaminants. *(Courtesy IBM Corporation)*

11

Computers Go
Solid

By 1950, the computer had been developed into the form we know today. The basic scientific and mathematical foundations were in place and had been utilized by technologists. The principles of operation of a computer were known and understood. The concepts of input-output, central processing, and memory storage were all reduced to practice. The basic principles of programming had been developed, the stored program concept implemented, and the potentiality of advanced computer languages perceived.

The only things that were to change were the nature of the components that went into a computer. Even in 1950, most of this basic technology had been developed.

A typical 1950 computer was a huge, hot, hungry machine with thousands of vacuum tubes, each one subject to failure. An army of technicians was required to keep both the computer and its environmental control system in operation. In order to get the computer to do what was desired, another army of programmers had to work out complex new connections on plugboards or create new instructions on punched paper tape, punch cards, or primitive magnetic tape. Even at its fastest, the vacuum tube computer of the early 1950s such as the IBM 701, operating at 2,200 multiplications per second, took an hour to solve a problem in aircraft design. Granted, this was considerably faster than the seven years it would have taken a single human aerodynamicist; but it was still slow, and the length of time required for the number crunching increased the possibility that a vacuum tube would fail and thus shut down the computer.

Because of all these factors, large general-purpose electronic digital computers were very expensive to buy and operate in 1950. Is it any wonder that people, especially computer specialists, didn't foresee the explosion of computer use that would take place in the next half of the twentieth century?

Not even the science-fiction writers of the time foresaw the consequences of the computer revolution, which hadn't really started to reach its stride yet. However, Arthur C. Clarke had written about the communications revolution, an integral part of the computer-created information revolution of today. There were many science-fiction stories about robots, and some of these did address some of the potential problems. Jack Williamson's novel *The Humanoids* looked into the consequences of perfect computerlike humanoid robots whose basic instruction was: "Serve and obey and guard men from harm." Isaac Asimov's stories about computerlike robots introduced "the three laws of robotics" in 1941. These had to be at the core of programming of all computers and automata or we would be in real trouble. Substitute the word *computer* for *robot,* and the reason becomes clear:

1. A robot may not injure a human being, or, through inaction, allow a human being to come to harm.
2. A robot must obey the orders given to it by human beings except where such orders would conflict with the first law.
3. A robot must protect its own existence as long as such protection does not conflict with the first or second law.

But nobody guessed that a computer would become small enough to wear as a wristwatch or would come to resemble a small television set with a typewriter keyboard in front.

The big breakthrough came with a device that would, for a time, replace the big, hot vacuum tube and demand less power.

The gadget came from Bell Laboratories in Murray Hill, New Jersey, where, as the R&D component of the AT&T Bell System, work was continually under way to improve telephone switching systems, as well as long-distance voice transmission.

Telegraphy and telephony, both "land-line" and "wireless," were the precursor technologies to electronics, which, following World War II, embraced both; it had already added television, radar, microwaves, and teletype. Before Dr. Lee De Forest developed the vacuum tube as an amplifier, solid devices utilizing single crystals had been used. Early wireless receivers used crystals of galena salts as detectors, and many people were introduced to the world of electronic wizardry by "crystal sets." Another early wireless detector was called a "coherer" and was a tube of iron filings that would, if continually disturbed, detect radio transmissions. Copper oxide and selenium rectifiers were widely used in electronics before 1960.

There is a class of metalloid elements known as "semiconductors," which will conduct electrons only under certain conditions. Galena salts happen to be naturally-occurring semiconductors that act like diodes, devices that conduct electricity only in one direction. Copper oxide and some selenium salts behave similarly. In World War II, semiconductor materials began to find new uses as radio frequencies increased beyond the capabilities of vacuum tubes to handle them. Russell S. Ohl discovered that crystal detectors were far more sensitive than vacuum tubes for the microwave and radar applications of World War II.

But in spite of more than half a century of experience with semiconductor or "solid state" electronic devices used as rectifiers of electricity, nobody knew how to make them amplify like a vacuum tube.

The answers began to come from theoretical physics, primarily the new quantum physics of Erwin Schrodinger in 1926 and Werner Heisenberg in 1927. There is no rational scientific theory behind quantum mechanics; it's primarily empirical, but it works. Albert Einstein initially objected to the principles of quantum mechanics, but grew to accept them, although he could never account for them with relativistic physics. In 1940, using quantum mechanics, Wilhelm Schottky proposed a theory for the semiconductor rectifier, although he couldn't explain such things as its dependence upon surface conditions. These were solved in 1947 by a theory of surface energy states proposed by Dr. John Bardeen.

This led very quickly to the development in December 1947 of the point-contact transistor amplifier by three Bell Labs men:

Dr. John Bardeen, Dr. William Houser Brattain, and Dr. William Bradford Shockley.

All three men had worked toward this discovery during their individual professional lives. They shared the Nobel Prize for solid-state physics in 1956. Bardeen went on from Bell Labs to a tenured professorship of physics at the University of Illinois, where he developed a theory of superconductivity. Brattain stayed at Bell Labs and developed theories of the surface properties of solids. We'll hear more about Shockley later.

Even today a transistor is viewed by many people—including some electrical engineers—as a bit of pure, out-and-out magic. This isn't a poor analysis of it—magic is a technology that one does not understand. And the scientific theory and technical knowledge behind a transistor is indeed complex and not as easy to understand as that of a steam engine, gasoline engine, or mechanical calculator. (However, even those commonplace technical achievements depend on such phenomena as combustion kinetics, which have little scientific basis.)

A transistor is one of a series of devices made up of metalloid or metallike materials known as "semiconductors." Some materials are conductors—copper and silver will readily conduct electricity. Others are nonconductors—rubber, ceramics, wood, among others, are insulators that won't permit the passage of electric current. Just as the word implies, semiconductors will or won't or will only partially conduct electricity, depending upon a wide variety of conditions.

The element germanium—symbol Ge, atomic number 32, atomic weight 72.59, discovered in 1886, named after Germany—is one such semiconductor material.

The element silicon—symbol Si, atomic number 19, atomic weight 28.086, discovered in 1823—is another one. Silicon is a member of the carbon family of elements and is the second most abundant element on earth, making up about one-fourth of the earth's crust. (Oxygen is number one and is present in half of the crust. No wonder—together with silicon, oxygen is part of ordinary sand.)

As Brattain, Bardeen, and Shockley discovered, the electrical characteristics of germanium (and silicon) can be altered by adding very slight amounts of impurities in a process that has come to be known as "doping." To give germanium an excess of electrons and therefore to turn it into an electron donor or "N-type" semiconductor, the doping material is the element anti-mony—symbol Sb, atomic number 51, atomic weight 121.75, discovered in 1450. To make germanium an electron acceptor or a "hole carrier" (a "hole" being a place where an electron should be but isn't), the dopant is the element indium—symbol In, atomic number 49, atomic weight 114.82, discovered in 1863, a member of the boron family.

Brattain, Bardeen, and Shockley's first transistor was what is now known as a "point-contact" transistor. It used two small wires in contact with a large base of doped germanium. The emitter and the collector act in an analogous fashion to the cathode and anode or plate of a vacuum tube, whereas the base acts in much the same manner as the grid in a De Forest audion or triode tube. This analogy is not precisely correct because other mechanisms involving electron and hole flow take place, but it's close enough to provide a basic description of the device. Just how the point-contact transistor worked is still obscure and controversial. It makes little difference at the moment, however, because this original, primitive transistor was quickly surpassed in performance by the diffused-junction transistor that came along in 1950 as a result of Shockley's work on the theory of semiconductor junctions of 1949.

The transistor and the rapid development of improved transistor types is an excellent example of what is known among technological forecasters as the "Hahn-Strassmann Point." This refers to the critical experiment in nuclear fission performed by Otto Hahn and Frantz Strassmann in Berlin in 1938. Until the Hahn-Strassman experiment, and the confirmation of its results by other physicists, nobody believed that nuclear fission could be artificially induced, and nobody knew how to do it. Afterward, dozens of other people around the world did it, too. And the field of nuclear energy progressed very quickly. The Hahn-Strassmann Point is that critical happening in any field of human activity that separates the impossible from the inevitable. Before the Hahn-Strassmann Point is reached, the future development of the field is uncertain; after it occurs, this development becomes a certainty and proceeds with alarming speed.

Not just *one* type of transistor was developed within the next few years. At least *five* came into existence.

The original point-contact transistor didn't offer much in

the way of improved performance over the best vacuum tubes of the day. One of its big problems was heat generated at the points of contact. Another was the limited-frequency response due to the slow velocities of electrons and holes through crystalline structure; in contrast, their velocities are at or near the speed of light in vacuum tubes. Some of the heat problems were solved by Shockley's development of the junction transistor. The limited-frequency response of the junction transistor was in turn partially solved by Shockley's field-effect transistor, or FET.

Although germanium was the base crystalline material of the early transistors, these units couldn't dissipate much heat without destroying themselves. The silicon-based transistor, coupled with a learning curve on how to keep silicon transistors cool with specially designed heat sinks, eventually overcame the heat problem. To some extent, excess heat, whether it comes from internal or external sources, is still a major problem in transistorized equipment today.

Solid-state electronics developed quickly in the 1950s. Hardly a month went by without the introduction of some new type or model transistor. General Electric was one of the first companies to become deeply involved in the manufacture of transistors with their ubiquitous 2N107 type. Philco and Zenith also became involved. But it wasn't until Motorola actually began mass production of transistors on assembly lines in the early 1960s that transistors started to become as commonplace as and cheaper than equivalent-performance vacuum tubes.

By 1960, transistors were not only outperforming vacuum tubes in most amplifying applications, but had created totally new products because of their increased sensitivity, small size, and reduced power requirements.

Transistors had an unforeseen side effect: their widespread use in a growing number of applications involving portable electronic equipment stimulated progress in the field of batteries. Although the LeClanche-type dry cell and the nickle-cadmium cell existed before the transistor, it wasn't until afterward that we got the alkaline battery, improvements in the LeClanche cell, and a host of new batteries such as the magnesium and lithium cells.

There is a strange, off-beat story to the development of the transistor that's another example of an invention ahead of its time.

The basic solid-state transistor was invented in 1926. On October 8, 1926, Dr. Julius Edgar Lilienfeld of Brooklyn, New York, filed for a United States patent on a "Method and Apparatus for Controlling Electric Currents." Dr. Lilienfeld had been a professor at the University of Liepzig in Poland, but had immigrated to the United States and become a U.S. citizen in 1935. His patent was issued on January 28, 1930, as U.S. Patent Number 1,745,175. It thoroughly and completely describes, along with drawings and wiring diagrams, an NPN junction transistor and its use in a multistage amplifier.

This might not seem unusual. There are a lot of strange patents issued every Tuesday by the U.S. Patent Office. Lilienfeld, however, didn't get just one patent on a solid-state amplifying device that looks unmistakably like a junction transistor, but *two* more patents. One of these, Patent Number 1,877,140, granted September 13, 1932, describes a multijunction NPPN or PNNP transistor. The other, Patent Number 1,900,018, granted March 7, 1933, shows an NPN transistor using cuprous sulfide and oxidized aluminum. In the latter, Lilienfeld also describes what electronic engineers would call a "reversed-bias P-N junction" to be used as a variable capacitor.

Dr. Lilienfeld died in 1963, long after Brattain, Bardeen, and Shockley had collected their Nobel Prizes for the development of a solid-state amplifying device previously described by Lilienfeld.

Why would these three patents be totally ignored for twenty or more years and the credit for inventing the transistor, along with international acclaim, lavished on someone else? When the Patent Office issues new patents each week, thousands of copies of each are sent around the world to subscribers. Thousands of patent attorneys research the Patent Office files constantly.

Lilienfeld's 1930 transistor patent wasn't hidden or suppressed. It was ignored. It wasn't needed. It was superfluous. Technology was moving in other directions, and the vacuum tube hadn't yet reached its limits of performance. All of the interest, all of the money, all of the industrial research, and all of the academic graduate research was aimed toward improvements in vacuum tube technology and scientific understanding of these devices. Nobody except a few obscure professors were thinking about surface effects, semiconduction, and the like. As a matter of fact, the scientific theories associated with quantum mechanics had just been announced, so nobody really knew that most of the semiconductor effects existed at all.

Lilienfeld's early discoveries should not be construed as casting any aspersions on the work of Brattain, Bardeen, and Shockley. These men were fortunate enough to be in the right place at the right time with the right discovery. They knew how their transistor might be used. They had a market for it. They had the means to communicate their discovery to others. And they had the clout of a very prestigious organization behind them.

But computer engineers didn't begin immediately to transistorize vacuum tube computers. In the first place, the early transistors didn't behave exactly like vacuum tubes. Transistors are primarily electric *current* devices, whereas vacuum tubes are electrical *voltage* units. In addition, the early transistors were expensive and heat sensitive, whereas vacuum tubes were cheap and rugged. Early transistors capable of operating at radio frequencies of about 30 megaHertz cost as much as $30, whereas most off-the-shelf vacuum tubes costing $3 could be used in 30mHz applications. It didn't last, however, once advanced transistor architecture and mass production got under way.

IBM claims to have developed the first automatic mass-production facility for transistors in Poughkeepsie, New York, in 1960. It was capable of producing and testing up to eighteen hundred transistors per hour. Automated mass production was one step in bringing transistor costs down to the level of vacuum tubes and, eventually, less. The next step was to improve the reliability and to reduce the reject rate, a task that was tackled by both IBM and Motorola.

It also took some time to develop transistors that acted as fast electron switches rather than as amplifiers, although AT&T began using transistors in their switching circuits in the 1950s.

This didn't mean that *nobody* was transistorizing computers, however. Probably the biggest and most popular electronic engineering task in the 1950s was to transistorize everything to the maximum extent possible, even though the resulting products didn't appear until far into the 1960s. The potential of the transistor was far too attractive to engineers. The fact that a transistor was only 1/200th the size of a vacuum tube and used only 1/100th of the power were attraction enough. Few thought then that the transistor would offer increased computer operating speeds as well.

In 1957, IBM introduced the IBM 608, the first all-transistor commercial calculator. It wasn't a full computer, but was comparable to a desktop adding machine. It didn't offer much in the way of improved performance over its vacuum tube counterpart, the IBM 607. And it was expensive; only ten of them were sold. But it broke ground for the 1959 IBM 1401, which was all transistorized and moderately priced. These small computers began to show up in banks, retail chains, and manufacturing plants. By 1965, more than ten thousand of them were sold, making it the most widely used computer up to that time.

NCR wasn't far behind. With a marketing philosophy derived from supplying cash registers to retail outlets, NCR was well positioned to introduce the electronic computer, vacuum tube or transistor, to a wide variety of commercial markets. In 1956, NCR introduced to banks the Post-Tronic machine for reading magnetic ledger cards and verifying posted accounts. In 1959, they went head-to-head with IBM with the NCR 304, a solid-state general business computer, followed in 1960 by the NCR 390 low-cost, mass-market computer.

The Burroughs Adding Machine Company was not to be left out. In 1953, it was renamed the Burroughs Corporation and, in 1956, acquired Electro-Data Corporation of Pasadena to obtain that firm's base in electronic computer technology.

This was indicative of a general trend in large corporations over the next quarter of a century and was nicknamed the "Harvard Business School Approach" to a company developing new technology. Actually, it didn't involve a company developing new technology at all, but acquiring it by purchase. The basic philosophy of the Harvard Business School Approach was that it is less expensive to buy new technology than to develop it. Let a small company take the risks and prove the technology, then buy the small company so that the successful risk takers become millionaires and the acquiring company risks nothing, just a little cash and some stock. The risk comes later when the big company tries to make the successful little company continue to work in the big company's environment.

Burroughs concentrated on business-oriented computer-like machines primarily for banks. In 1961, they put on the market a series of small B200 medium-scale solid-state computers, as well as the B5000 solid-state modular data-processing system, which was touted as the most advanced business and scientific computer available because it featured automatic multiprogramming and the use of compiler languages, a first in the industry.

But the big advance created by transistors was in component packaging. IBM, NCR, and Burroughs had all developed plug-in modules for vacuum tube computers. IBM went a step further in modularization for transistors by pioneering the use of the printed circuit card.

Printed circuits were compact, easier to produce, easier to repair (if you followed certain new techniques specific to printed circuit boards), and less expensive. A nonconducting thin sheet of plastic, phenolic, or fiberglass was used as the mounting substrate. On one side, electrical connections between components were first "printed" in electrically conductive material. Later, plastic boards plated on one or both sides with copper and coated with a photosensitive material were used; the electronic circuit connections of these later boards were then photographically etched, leaving conductive paths. Components such as transistors, capacitors, and resistors were mounted on the board with their connecting wires passing through holes in the board. These connections were then soldered either by dip soldering or, for small production runs, manually with a soldering iron. Printed circuit boards later came to have their connectors etched on as part of the circuit, eliminating the need to provide connecting wires between the board and its main computer chassis. The cards were plugged into large "gates" or "buses," which swung out or could be pulled out for easier maintenance. Many modern personal computers still use this technology, now inexpensive and still very reliable.

An IBM engineer presented this viewpoint: "The key wasn't only the transistor card, it was the whole circuit packaging system—the rack panel, the gate, the industrial design, the memories, the power supplies. Everything had to be standardized to assure high, *predictable* reliability, at reasonable cost, machine after machine after machine."

In 1960, using transistors and printed circuit technologies, IBM engineers built a semiexperimental computer named

"Stretch" because they felt that they were "stretching" the technology in building it. IBM sold eight of them starting in 1961. Each Stretch contained 150,000 transistors and was 75 times faster than its vacuum tube counterparts. It also featured innovations such as "look-ahead" programming to prepare for coming work in the program, the overlapping/pipelining of instructions, automatic operation under the control of advanced operating systems, and the introduction of the 8-bit byte or word. Although its high speed helped in the study of long-range weather forecasting and nuclear power plant design, Stretch didn't measure up to its initial design objectives. But it did prove out many of the design features of the advanced transistorized computers then under development at IBM. Many computer engineers considered it the predecessor of the highly successful IBM System 360, which was another generation in the future but only four years down the line.

This in itself is significant. The development of a generation of computers had been shortened from more than a decade to a matter of four years. It also meant that computers themselves were becoming obsolescent in years rather than decades, a difficult problem that the computer industry would have to face eventually lest they be accused of engaging in "planned obsolescence."

12

The False Dawn

In 1960, the idea that a private individual might someday own his own computer was laughable. In the first place, even if some early-day millionaire computer hacker had been able to afford such a general-purpose machine, he would have had problems getting it to do anything, in spite of the beginnings of modern programming technology such as the operating system. Computers were still reserved for organizations that had problems in handling and processing large amounts of data—banks, insurance companies, the federal government, and scientific and academic institutions. The data-processing requirements of the Acme Widget Company, with gross annual sales of $500,000, could still be handled by the classic clerk, bookkeeper, and accountant armed with a ten-column or ten-key desktop adding machine, often printing out the entries and results on a roll of paper. Such machines were those made by Marchant, Monroe, Friden, or Victor. As for ordinary people, they could get along quite well using a pencil and paper, although this ancient method of scrivening didn't give them as much control over their numbers as they would gain a mere decade later.

But the 1960s heard the swan song of the desk calculator or adding machine. Marchant, Monroe, and Friden were gone by the 1970s, merged into or acquired by other electronic computer companies, or in receivership. New companies run by a fresh batch of people emerged.

It might seem that in 1960 there were only four major firms in the growing computer industry (the business machine business)—IBM, NCR, Remington Rand, and Burroughs. Not so, although they were probably the biggest. The introduction of the transistor on a large scale, in electronics and in computers, triggered the formation of a host of new little companies and encouraged some Fortune 500 firms to test the waters of the computer field.

Some of these large firms were looking for diversification and, listening to the graduates of the Harvard Business School, tried to buy into the computer industry and obtain the technology and marketing expertise through acquisition.

Others decided that computers were nothing more than a specialized product quite similar to the others in their product lines and that they could simply diversify from within, using their good image and already powerful marketing departments to penetrate what they perceived to be a fairly straightforward and existing marketplace.

As might be expected, some of them made it and some of them didn't. The reasons some did make it are various, with a few being completely illogical and totally unanticipated. The ones that failed did so for similar reasons. The smart outfits that failed in spite of all their pomp, power, and friendships with investment analysts took the advice of the successful Las Vegas high-rolling gambler: "Quit while you're winning and support a friend."

General Electric did just that.

Formed in the 1880s around the electrical inventions of Thomas Alva Edison (who initially kept the lamp business to himself), General Electric is one of the few United States corporations that has not only remained high on the Forbes 100 list, but has managed to remain there, period. It has never dropped below number 11 on the list. Considering all of the changes and the enormous amount of technical progress that has occurred in the past century, this is a remarkable achievement. Of 209 companies that have appeared on the Forbes 100 list since 1917, only 34 of them (7.52 percent) have remained on the list for sixty years. Fully a third of the companies on the 1917 Forbes 100 were not on the 1977 list.

The GE phenomenon hasn't been fully analyzed, but it may be due partially to two GE strong points: continual corporate support of both basic research and product development, and a corporate marketing philosophy that is thorough, flexible, and realistic. GE has expanded and diversified primarily from within, and it has been quick to grasp new applications and new markets for technological improvements to its existing product lines.

General Electric was the first company to buy and install a Remington Rand UNIVAC 1 in 1954. By 1956, GE had developed its own electronic computer capability to the point where it landed the largest-ever contract in the commercial computer field—$60 million—for the development and installation of its Electronic Recording Method of Accounting (ERMA) in thirteen Bank of America locations in California. To perform the requirements of this contract, GE opened its first computer department in Phoenix, Arizona, in the same year. ERMA's banking debut took place in San Jose, California, in 1958, right in the middle of the embryonic Silicon Valley entrepreneurial companies. By 1960, from its experience with ERMA, GE had developed the GE-210 computer, which became standardized by the American Bankers Association. In fact, U.S. Patent Number 3,000,000 was issued and assigned to GE; it covered the Magnetic Ink Character Recognition system developed to read ERMA computer printouts. The strange-looking numbers that appear on the bottom margin of checks today came from that GE development. By 1964, GE was on a roll in the computer business. It set up Bull-GE and Olivetti-General Electric to exploit the European computer market and began shipping the new GE-400 family of medium-size computers for banking, business, manufacturing, and special-purpose applications. And GE set up the first computer time-sharing experiments at Dartmouth College, where sixteen terminals were installed for student and faculty use. A third-generation computer, the GE-600 series, went into production in Phoenix in 1965 and had such competitive features as multiprogramming and multiprocessing. In Italy, Olivetti-GE introduced the GE-115 small-scale computer. In the same year, the world's largest advanced large-scale time-sharing system, the GE-645 Multics, went on line for Project MAC at MIT and Bell Labs. GE also inaugurated time-sharing services for commercial customers. Time-sharing services were opened in Paris, Milan, The Hague, Brussels,

Cologne, Copenhagen, Stockholm, Acton, Manchester, and Sydney in 1968.

Then something happened.

For some reason, GE decided to bail out of the computer business just as it had pulled out of the rocket business some ten years before. This decision may have come from either the financial people or the marketing people. Probably a little bit of both, since GE has rarely divorced marketing from any part of its highly diversified business. Perhaps the company wasn't making any money with the Phoenix computer division in what was becoming a highly competitive, price-sensitive market-place.

There is an apocryphal story that I first heard in a market-ing seminar conducted by GE-trained marketing men that may offer some clue to what took place. A meat-packing company decided it would use some of its waste by-product in a new line of dog food. This required only minor changes in the plant procedure. The packaging people came up with an attractive name and an eye-catching package and label. The advertising department worked up an outstanding multimedia ad campaign along with self-liquidating premiums and other buyer incen-tives. The sales department nailed down huge orders from the major supermarket chains. And the company shipped on sched-ule. The sales department sat back and waited for the reorders to pour in. They didn't pour in. Product returns poured in instead. Cases and cases of dog food came back. After an ini-tial spate of consumer purchases, it wouldn't sell. It seems the meat-packing company had overlooked something: dogs wouldn't eat it.

Apparently, in spite of all the marketing power of General Electric, they couldn't achieve the market position they believed they should have against IBM, NCR, Burroughs, and the oth-ers. So they did the obvious thing: they quit while they were winning and they started supporting a friend—lots of them—by providing many of the components and peripherals that didn't entail such high risks and require so much market preparation.

On October 1, 1970, GE sold their entire computer opera-tion, including the Phoenix plant, to Honeywell, Inc., of Minne-apolis, Minnesota. GE, however, retained a computer service operation, the General Electric Information Services Division, to supply computerized services to a wide variety of industrial customers, large and small. And GE had supplied a great deal of the computerized prelaunch checkout equipment for the Apollo lunar landing program. The GE Automatic Checkout Equipment (ACE) did in seconds what would have taken technicians hours or days to inspect.

Whether or not GE made the right long-term decision in the domestic computer marketplace remains to be seen, but Honeywell has done very well with their acquired GE property. They should have, because they were well equipped to take it over. Even according to the GE marketing principles, Honeywell had everything going for them.

Honeywell, Inc., is now in its second century, and even when it acquired GE's computer division, it was well equipped from a historic viewpoint to expand its activities in the computer field. In a manner of speaking, Honeywell had always been in the computer industry, since it was formed in 1883 by Alfred M. Butz, a Minneapolis inventor who'd developed the first automatic furnace thermostat for domestic use. A household thermostat, as we saw earlier, is a robot or automaton. It's dumb, it's stupid, but it does exactly what it's been told to do without failure for years on end. The Butz Thermo-Electric Regulator Company underwent a surprisingly large number of name changes before it emerged as the Minneapolis Heat Regulator Company in 1912. Meanwhile, Mark C. Honeywell formed Honeywell Heating Specialties Company in Wabash, Indiana, to build hot water heaters. The two outfits got together in 1927, when the Minneapolis company was the leading manufacturer of thermostatic and other controls for coal-fired domestic furnaces and the Honeywell firm was the leader in oil-burner controls. The result was the Minneapolis Honeywell Regulator Company, incorporated in Delaware but headquartered in Minneapolis.

"Minny-Honey," as it was long known in the trade, kept expanding its line of heat controls, eventually diversifying into industrial hydraulic and pneumatic controls by means of acquisitions. In 1940, Minny-Honey took on its first defense contract, making precision optical sights and tank periscopes. It got into the computer business in a sort of sideways fashion via its industrial control expertise, which led to the development of the

Army's Computer-1 airplane autopilot during World War II. An autopilot, like a thermostat, is a stupid computer whose program is simple: using feedback from the machine to determine its past and current situation and condition, it keeps the machine doing what it's supposed to be doing according to the instructions given the autopilot by a human operator.

After World War II, having established considerable experience in automatic controls, both military and domestic, Minneapolis-Honeywell began to build up its industrial measurement and control capabilities, again through acquisition. But because there was a fine line between the simple industrial, military, and domestic control systems and computer systems—one being classed as "logical automata" and the other as "computing automata"—the company slowly acquired expertise in electronics, especially in solid-state devices. In 1954, a Transistor Division was established because the Research Laboratory had developed an important breakthrough: a transistor capable of handling and dissipating large amounts of electrical power, something that the early germanium transistors couldn't handle.

The first excursion directly into computer technology was made in 1955 when Minny-Honey and Raytheon entered into a joint venture by creating Datamatic Corporation in Newton, Massachusetts, to design, develop, and produce large-scale computer systems. In 1957, Raytheon pulled a GE trick: they bailed out of computers by selling their interest in Datamatic to Minny-Honey. The move may have been premature because in 1957 the first Datamatic D-1000 computer was installed to handle the growing flood of data converging on Blue Cross/Blue Shield of Michigan.

The computer business at Minneapolis-Honeywell kept growing and bred some interesting offshoots. Honeywell got into ballistic missile and space vehicle guidance systems, basically autopilots with preprogrammed computers to guide them rather than human beings. In 1960, the Honeywell Model 400 computer could handle six thousand arithmetic operations per second. By 1962, with the Model 1800, Honeywell was definitely in the computer business, alongside IBM and the rest of the pack. By 1963, an indication of the extent of the competition (reminiscent in some ways of the current situation) was the

Honeywell Model 200, which boasted five times the processing speed of the competitive IBM 1401. On top of that, the Honeywell "liberator concept" was a cross-programming translation program that allowed the IBM 1401 software to run in the Honeywell 200.

Minny-Honey disappeared in April 1964, when the corporate name was shortened to Honeywell, Inc. In 1967, Honeywell bought into more computer technology through its purchase of the Computer Control Company. And the year before acquiring GE's computer division, Honeywell's Computer Control Division announced its 316 minicomputer, the fourth in a series of compatible machines.

Maintaining its competitive streak, Honeywell brought out the Model 8200 general-purpose solid-state computer in 1965; this new product could run with the software from the Series 200 and Models 800/1800. Even then, the sales carrot amounted to a hardware product that was faster and smaller while at the same time compatible with existing programming software, even if it was the competitor's software!

IBM hadn't been dormant in the marketplace while all this was going on. In addition to transistorizing at a great rate and developing new and faster memory storage devices like the magnetic core array, IBM sought out new applications where handling and processing of large amounts of data were becoming both commonplace and problematic. One of these areas was commercial aviation.

Starting in 1958, the commercial airlines of the world underwent enormous changes. Pan American ordered twenty Boeing 707 and twenty Douglas DC-8 jet airliners, thereby triggering the most intense reequipment period ever experienced in that industry. Suddenly, airlines had on their hands aircraft that could operate twelve to sixteen hours a day in the air carrying up to 179 passengers at 80 percent the speed of sound. This was an enormous increase in the number of seats available each day, especially as each airline tried to outdo its competitors on such popular routes as New York to Los Angeles. Knowing how many seats were available on what flight, how many seats had been sold, who required special attention, special meals, or other types of special services caused major and overwhelming bookkeeping problems.

IBM set up a joint program with American Airlines to computerize the passenger reservation system with the first large, high-speed commercial computerized communications network operating in "real time"—handling transactions as they actually occurred regardless of where they took place. It took six years of intensive research. But the SABRE computerized reservation system went on line for American Airlines in 1962. With SABRE, twelve hundred computer terminals across the United States could feed data into the basic computer located in Tarrytown, New York, and in turn receive data back. Reservations could be made on a first-come, first-serve basis. One of the original computer disk memories kept track of more than a million passenger records. It allowed an American Airlines reservations clerk to make or change a traveler's airline reservations in a few seconds. It was obviously a success, forcing other airlines to acquire their own computerized systems. These various systems were, in turn, eventually linked to one another into one master overall airline reservation service with many computers and thousands of terminals talking to one another. Eventually, this basic reservation service was expanded to include assignment of seat locations, rental car reservations, and hotel/motel reservations for the traveler as well.

But not all the efforts to computerize America, much less conservative Europe, were successful.

In the 1960s, computers had taken on an aura of infallibility. More than ever, they were considered superelectronic brains that couldn't make a mistake. But troubles began because all of the ins and outs of computerization hadn't been thought through and because many areas of the technology simply weren't up to the job yet. It gave rise to the most common excuse of the late twentieth century: "Computer error." Or the most common excuse for a delay: "Our computer's down." Companies in the computer business began to run up against resistance in the marketplace. Up to then, they'd placed computers in established markets where the user's main preoccupation was counting—banks, insurance companies, and the like. Now computers had been installed in many businesses that had never had them before but had fallen prey to the computerization fad.

Two problems immediately surfaced: the computers could

do many more things and provide far more data than the customers thought they needed at that time, and staffs of computer programmers had to be retained on practically a full-time basis to debug the programs. The computers produced "wall-to-wall" data, provided the programs would run that day.

The reaction to the premature computerization of American industry was nowhere more forcibly expressed than in Robert Townsend's 1970 best-seller *Up the Organization:* ". . . Most of the computer technicians that you're likely to meet or hire are complicators, not simplifiers. They're trying to make it look tough. Not easy. They're building a mystique, a priesthood, their own mumbo-jumbo ritual to keep you from knowing what they—and you—are doing."

At the time, programming wasn't that easy, and programmers didn't deserve the chastisement Townsend laid on them. In spite of the fact that operating systems had been around for about ten years and stored programs were a commonplace thing in computers, there was little prepackaged software. Nearly every application required customized programs. Programmers had to rely upon one of several programming approaches.

They could program in "machine language," which is extremely difficult and requires instructions for *every* step to be converted to the binary number system understood by the computer. This machine language program must then be entered step by step. It's so complex that hardly a machine language program can be developed, entered, and run without some sort of bug cropping up. Debugging takes a lot of time because, unlike writing the program from scratch on a clean sheet of paper, so to speak, the programmer knows that there's a mistake in there *somewhere* and that it's up to him to find it— speaking the machine's own language in the process, of course.

Or a programmer could use one of the existing computer languages as a basis. IBM had developed what is now known as a "high-level" program language as opposed to a low-level language that operates closer to machine language. This was called FORTRAN, an acronym for FORmula TRANslation. It first became available in 1957 and enabled scientists and engineers to talk to a computer in a language that was halfway between standard mathematical notation and machine language. An equation could be stated in familiar symbols with FORTRAN. An example is:

Mathematics: $D = B^2 - 4AC$
FORTRAN: $D = B^{**}2 - 4^*A^*C$

Another high-level computer language and one that is still used primarily in business is COBOL (Common Business Oriented Language), whose development was partially worked out by pioneer programmer Grace Hopper. Probably the most-used computer language of 1984 is BASIC in all its various forms, invented by John Kemeny and Thomas Kurtz at Dartmouth College.

Or a programmer could perhaps adapt an existing program developed for an analogous application elsewhere. But in 1970, this wasn't easy to do. There wasn't a huge library of software to call upon.

Two developments occurring in reasonably rapid sequence solved some of the problems of computerizing business that created the "false dawn" of 1970 and led to Townsend's indictment of the computer. They also placed an enormous burden on programmers to come up with the necessary software that would exploit the new developments and enable the computer revolution to continue because, even with thousands of transistorized computers in use, things hadn't really started to move yet.

13

How Creative
Was the Valley?

By 1960, the computer industry and the state of the art in computer technology had grown to such a magnitude that it becomes practically impossible to write a chronological history including every occurrence of importance. While exploitation of computer technology for the marketplace was going on in one place, development of new technology was going on elsewhere, and research into the scientific foundations and new ideas was proceeding at yet other places. This is still happening today.

Using hindsight, it's always possible to try to learn why certain ideas and concepts succeeded and others didn't. But there's enough of a story in those that made it without considering those that didn't, except for special instances where a failure had a strong impact on future developments. And, as the history of the computer revolution makes abundantly clear, it's always a story of people making the right guesses and being in the right place at the right time with the right new technology—plus knowing how to sell it.

While the giants of the computer industry were busily at work exploiting the transistor on the printed circuit board for solid-state computers, developing new memory and data-storage devices, working on new input and output devices, and thrashing through the early software programs, the Santa Clara Valley of central California and its academic capital, Stanford University, were areas that were far from quiescent.

In 1955, Shockley, of the trio of Bardeen, Brattain, and Shockley (inventors of the transistor), left Bell Labs to relocate in Palo Alto, California, as chief of the new Shockley Semiconductor Laboratories of Beckmann Instruments Company. This lab was set up in the new Stanford Industrial Park located near the university, a prototype for similar research and industrial parks that sprang up around the country in the next twenty years. A far cry from the crowded brick factory buildings surrounded by smoke stacks—the usual nesting grounds of industrial R&D labs until that time—this visionary nurturing place of high technology included a campuslike atmosphere of widely separated buildings, grass and trees, and a general academic atmosphere touched with the urgency of commercial R&D. Light high-tech industry was also encouraged to locate in such industrial research parks. Behind the research labs and small companies came a phalanx of supporting operations to provide parts, supplies, and services. The industrial research park offered the atmosphere and surroundings of academia without the requirement of teaching or the need to "publish or perish." The success of the research park idea is apparent to anyone familiar with the high-tech industrial environment and "Theory Z" company management policies thirty years later.

Well aware of the technical problems of germanium-based transistors—low power-handling and dissipation capabilities, sensitivity to temperature extremes, difficulty and expense of production, high reject rates, and other quality-control problems—Shockley wanted to work on silicon-based transistors that promised to eliminate some of these shortcomings. Shockley was a leader. He could persuade others to do what he wanted them to do and leave them not only doing it but liking it. He had to be an outstanding research manager because riding herd over any group of brilliant, clever, creative R&D people requires special leadership talents quite unlike those of a military general or the chief executive officer of a large corporation.

Shockley picked Palo Alto because it was already an electronics center. Professor Frederick Emmons Terman was there, and his Stanford Electronics Research Laboratory was an educational resource that helped the university turn out some of the best electronic engineers in the world. Terman's many textbooks on various aspects of electronics are still widely used at the university level.

In Palo Alto, Shockley gathered around him a cadre of gifted electronics engineers, specialists, and technicians he'd hand-picked from big companies and prominent universities. To get some of these people, he had to use attractive bait. The privilege of working with a Nobel laureate wasn't one of them, because he was not to receive the Nobel Prize with Bardeen and Brattain until 1956. The various bits and pieces of the bait used by Shockley to lure these creative people were many and should be noted by those who want to set up shop in any area of emerging high technology.

The entire Santa Clara Valley south of San Francisco was then an extremely attractive place to live, an ecological paradise at the northwest edge of what came to be known as the Sun Belt. Joel Garreau considers it to be part of what he calls "Ecotopia" in his book *The Nine Nations of North America*. It has a climate similar to that of France's Cote d'Azur and is, indeed, one of the few places in the world that has such a Mediterranean climate with ample rainfall and temperatures moderated by the close proximity of large bodies of water. If the ground shook occasionally because of the San Andreas fault, it was no worse than the threat of tornadoes and severe weather elsewhere in the Midwest and East. In addition to sunshine, there was rarely any snow. The nearby presence of Stanford University gave people an opportunity to continue their formal education if desired, as well as providing a continual new supply of fresh scientists and engineers. The university's research facilities could also be marshalled to tackle the problems of basic research that always underlie any fast-moving technology. Contrary to common belief, high technology that's moving ahead very rapidly always leads science. In this sort of situation, scientists are the people who come along after the technologists and try to learn by research why something the technologists developed works in the first place.

But the big problem with any industrial research activity is that it will always produce far more output than the company— any company, even AT&T, GE, or Exxon—can ever hope to absorb. Bell Labs and other corporations have handled this by selling off or licensing what they feel they can't use for at least ten years or for as long as the patent position remains strong. Some corporate executives, when hit by this technology shock, have reacted in the opposite manner: They have cut back the personnel or budget of the lab so that it doesn't produce so much output. But worst of all is when tech-shocked executives have simply ignored what their R&D lab people have done and then vacillated over what to do about all the wonderful new corporate research discoveries. The new high-tech product proposals usually don't resemble any of the company's current products, and the marketing department has no idea what the real market is or how to sell the new technology products. And usually, the marketing department simply doesn't want to spend the time and money to develop new markets.

But the primary result of this habit of industrial R&D labs to produce more than the company can use is the creation of a gamelike situation often known as "musical laboratories," a version of musical chairs played by bright research people with the personnel departments of other local firms and within the quiet politics of local chapters of ASME, IEEE, ASCE, and other professional societies. Brilliant people whose work has been ignored quit and go across the street, where they hope their ideas will be more warmly received.

Or they say to hell with big business, quit, mortgage everything they own, borrow every penny they can from family and friends, and start making their ignored new device in their garage. Nine out of ten fail. The tenth ends up a multimillionaire within ten years. That doesn't keep the other nine from starting out because, at the beginning, no one knows who's going to be successful, and everyone sincerely believes he or she's the one. It's called "private enterprise."

This massive overproduction of ideas, technology, and new products is exactly what happened to the Shockley Semiconductor Laboratories. Beckmann couldn't absorb or didn't want the total output of the lab. In 1959, some of Shockley's bright people started to leave.

One of these was Robert R. Noyce, who went across the street (in the literal sense) and got the backing of Fairchild Camera and Instrument Company to start Fairchild Semiconductor in Mountain View, a few miles south of Palo Alto. Robert Noyce had a big idea for a very little device.

So did Jack Kilby at Texas Instruments, Inc. (TI), in Dallas, Texas.

Robert Noyce at Fairchild and Jack Kilby at TI coinvented the integrated circuit (IC) in 1959. It took about a decade for the IC to find its way into computers in a big way, but when it did, the results were striking.

The basic operating element in any electronic device is a subatomic particle, the electron. It's so small that it sometimes acts like a particle and at other times behaves as though it were a light wave. This puzzles scientists but doesn't bother engineers, who simply use the characteristics of the electron and don't worry too much about what it is. True, the behavior of an electron as either a particle or a wave often enters into the basic design of some solid-state devices, but it's not necessary to know what an electron is, much less what it looks like, in order to make it useful. It's very small and very light. The mass of an electron was once estimated to be only 1/1837th that of a single atom of hydrogen. But because the electron is so small its mass is related to its energy according to the famous Einstein equation $E = mc^2$. It's impossible to think of an electron's size because of this close relationship between energy and matter on the subatomic scale and because the electron can act as both a particle and a wave.

Nearly all electronic devices thus far have manipulated huge numbers of electrons even at the highest microwave and radar frequencies where one might tend to believe that on-off times of such components as transistors might let only one or two electrons pass. The ultimate goal of having the movement of a single electron constitute a discrete signal in a computer or communications device hasn't been achieved yet, although it will become a reality within a surprisingly few years. Be that as it may, the basic element of electronics is the electron, usually in large numbers right now. The most obvious path toward building electronic devices that operate with electrons as signal carriers is to reduce the size of electronic devices.

The components used to manipulate the miniscule electron are, by comparison, incredibly huge, even with the current state of the art—wires and even transistors, for example, to say nothing of other components such as resistors and capacitors.

The long-term trend in electronic equipment has been to continually reduce its size, which in turn reduces its power requirements, thereby producing less waste energy in the form of heat and making the equipment more energy efficient. (Energy efficiency was a goal in the electronics industry long before it became a popular buzzword in our society.)

The transistor was a step toward the ultimate in miniaturization. But components such as resistors and capacitors, which are absolutely necessary in any electronic circuit, weren't appreciably reduced in size when the transistor became part of the state of the art.

Printed circuits helped reduce circuit dimensions. All necessary electronic components could be mounted on a thin phenolic or fiberglass board, the connecting wires etched, photodeposited, or vacuum deposited on the board surface, and the individual components mounted on the board one by one, their electrical leads being thermally soldered to the deposited wiring to complete the electrical paths or circuits.

But most of a tiny transistor, even the smallest available discrete transistor, amounts to the outer shell of metal or plastic plus the connecting wires. The actual electronic performance of a transistor takes place in a microscopic piece of slightly impure germanium or silicon in which the nature and amounts of impurities are carefully controlled in various parts of the piece during manufacture.

Quality control has been a constant problem with transistors. When transistors are made by the thousands on automated production lines, the performance of individual transistors can vary widely from unit to unit even within a production batch, to say nothing of the sort of variations that can occur from batch to batch. Much of the work in transistor technology in the 1950s and early 1960s was devoted to the nitpicking task of quality control to insure reliable, predictable performance, transistor to transistor.

And when transistors and other electronic components are soldered onto printed circuit (PC) boards, an individual board may not perform to specifications because of the inevitable variations in performance of its individual components. The universe as a whole works on statistical principles, and any large collection of items will have characteristics that fall on the normal distribution curve, which is shaped like a bell. A lot of effort has gone into reducing transistors from points along a normal bell-shaped distribution curve to a single point—this is quality control. However, the variation in performance from PC board to PC board can be reduced no further than the variations in performance of individual components on the board, and it's patently impossible to make *anything* without a variation of some sort from unit to unit.

But when Noyce and Kilby looked at a printed circuit board and brought what they saw together with what they knew about how transistors themselves are made, it became obvious to both of them independently that entire electronic circuits could be manufactured in much the same way that transistors are made: by *growing* or *plating* them onto a support layer known as a "substrate." A complete electronic circuit could be built up by a succession of layers of circuit components made up of elements of varying electronic properties—semiconductor characteristics, electrical resistance, electrical capacitance, etc.

Without going into boring technical details that involve as much chemistry as physics, the basic IC is built on a uniform chip or small piece of doped silicon much like a silicon transistor base. The silicon chip is, at this stage of IC manufacture, a tiny segment of a larger wafer from a single silicon crystal called a "boule." Hundreds of silicon wafers for depositing IC materials are cut from a single boule, and hundreds of chips are in turn eventually cut from a single wafer after the integrated circuit has been constructed on it. Impurities such as antimony, indium, gallium, and other "rare earth" elements (so-named because they are indeed rare on earth) and common elements such as aluminum are introduced onto the chip in very precise locations. Usually this is done by diffusion, which is analogous to organic growth, and by vacuum deposition. The geometry of the plane surface of the circuit on the chip is determined by photographically masking off certain areas, applying photochemical techniques, and laying down a coating of insulating oxide. Certain areas of the oxide coating are then opened up to allow the formation of interconnections between sections on the chip. Once the electronic circuit, with its transistors, resistors, capacitors, coils, and connections, is formed on a chip, this circuit is absolutely identical to the hundred or so other circuits that have been simultaneously formed on the other chips on the same wafer. They have been subjected to the same environmental conditions, temperatures, atmospheres, chemicals, etc., during formation, and there's an excellent probability that each will be as good as its neighbor. One of the factors that can cause chips to be rejected by quality-control inspectors is imperfection in the silicon crystal structure of the wafer itself. This is one of the things that's behind the desire to make near-perfect semiconductor crystals aboard the NASA space shuttle in the zero-gravity of orbital space. Such space crystals promise to permit both larger IC chips as well as lower reject rates. General Electric, whose researchers have looked into this matter, believe that the reject rate could be lowered so much that it would reduce the price of an IC by a factor of ten.

Each chip is then cut from the wafer, and the hairlike electrical wire leads that will tie it to the outside world are attached under a microscope. Today, most of this is done by robots, which can perform much finer microscopic work than human beings. Humans monitor the operation. Each IC is then encapsulated in a flat epoxy plastic enclosure with a plethora of connecting pins coming out along both long sides of it.

Thus, an IC is really nothing more than a "little black box," but a much smaller and more complex little black box than people ever thought possible when that term came into use during World War II.

Most of this manufacturing process is almost identical to that used to make transistors. Since integrated circuits could be made using existing transistor technology, a lot of old companies became IC manufacturers, along with newer companies. Both Fairchild and Texas Instruments produced ICs, along with old-timers such as Motorola and RCA and such newcomers as National Semiconductor.

A typical IC of the mid-1960s was the RCA CA3000, which was one of a family of more than forty RCA integrated circuit products available in electronic stores all over the country. It was intended for use as an amplifier and contained five transistors, two diodes, and eleven resistors. Packaged in a standard "TO-5" transistor case with ten leads coming out of the base, the CA3000 was no larger than a single transistor and weighed a fraction of an ounce. It would do the same electronics job as a discrete-component transistorized amplifier mounted on a three-by-four-inch PC board weighing an ounce and a half; or the same job as a vacuum tube amplifier using "miniature" tubes, assembled in an aluminum box measuring three by four by four inches and weighing nearly six ounces. The vacuum tube amplifier required either a very large battery or AC power supply, whereas the transistorized PC would work with a transistor radio battery. The CA3000 IC would operate with a battery no larger than what is now required for a digital quartz watch.

The IC created as much of a revolution as the transistor. Suddenly, within the span of less than a decade, it became possible to purchase an IC that contained a tested and working electronic circuit that would do just about anything required of an electronic circuit. There were audio, DC, video, IF, r-f, and operational amplifiers. An electronics buff could buy well-designed and tested oscillators, phase detectors, mixers, and arrays for incorporation directly into amateur, professional, research, test, and commercial electronic products.

The IC all but eliminated the profession of electronic circuit designer, just as the transistor practically wiped out the need for vacuum tube engineers.

The first ICs had only a few transistors. By 1969, however, Large Scale Integration or LSI chips became available. The engineers had been at it again and extended the technology to enable them to cram dozens of ordinary ICs onto a single chip, taking no more space than an ordinary IC. LSI chips containing hundreds of transistors became available. Complete radio transmitters and receivers, hi-fi stereo amplifiers, tone and frequency generators, video line bar and spot generators, color video burst generators, and a host of other complex devices were designed and produced on LSI chips.

Furthermore, because these LSI chips were so small, they were also very fast. It might take as much as a millionth of a second for a signal to go through an ordinary silicon transistor, but the signal transit time through an IC was as short as half a billionth of a second. The frequency response—a term that had suddenly come to have considerably less meaning than it had had a quarter of a century before, in the days of vacuum tubes— suddenly expanded from DC to the multimegaHertz range.

IC engineers also incorporated other obvious circuits into monolithic IC modules—computer gates, logic modules, memory modules, and a host of other circuits used in digital computers. The early versions of these computer IC chips, like their counterparts in other electronic fields, contained only a few transistors and were designed to replace specific circuits such as flip-flops for binary logic, various individual logic circuits such as *and, or,* and *nor* gates, buffers, and so forth.

The stage was thus set for the next big basic technological breakthrough, the one that suddenly brought the computer revolution out of the laboratory and counting house and into nearly every business and every home.

14

Working on the Edge of Disaster

In the history of the computer revolution, there have been some people who have been more than just scientists, mathematicians, engineers, or managers. They've done more than one thing. And the things they've done have shaped the course of the revolution that followed afterward. Among these multifaceted pioneers were Dr. Herman Hollerith, John H. Patterson, Thomas J. Watson (both Senior and Junior), Dr. John von Neumann, and Dr. William B. Shockley. True, other people have come on the scene and done great things, but then they have vanished into obscurity. Not these men. And not a growing cadre of younger men. Nor can we anticipate that there is an end to the list in sight.

Among them is Dr. Robert Norton Noyce, mentioned earlier, who founded Fairchild Semiconductor in 1957 in Mountain View, California. There, as we've seen, he was the coinventor, with Jack Kilby (Texas Instruments), of the integrated circuit chip.

Noyce stayed with Fairchild until 1968, when he grew weary of what he considered to be poor management policies and procedures within Fairchild Camera and Instrument's semiconductor division. He had risen to the position of general manager, vice-president, and then group vice-president of Fairchild. Along with several other managers at Fairchild, he felt that innovation was being stifled by too many high-level management meetings during which operational and product decisions were made with little apparent input from the working-level people. He later said during an interview published in the *Harvard Business Review:* "In the Fairchild situation, I simply felt that I couldn't leave and relax, which is a stupid way to run your life." He wanted to start a company that would operate in a new mode compatible with the changed world of high technology.

Gordon E. Moore, a long-time friend and close associate, shared Noyce's outlooks. He had gotten his Ph.D. in both chemistry and physics at Cal Tech in 1954 and had been one of Shockley's bright young transistor researchers in Palo Alto. He had left Shockley with Noyce to form Fairchild Semiconductor. He too saw the potential of the emerging LSI semiconductor technology. Along with Noyce, he was disturbed that Fairchild seemed to be lagging because its management took so long to make a decision and was so resistant to change.

The two of them approached Arthur Rock, the venture capitalist from San Francisco who had put together the money for earlier high-tech firms such as Scientific Data Systems and the huge conglomerate Teledyne. According to Noyce, it wasn't difficult. "We really never had any trouble getting money," he recalled in 1980. "It may shock a lot of people to find this out, but we never wrote a business plan, never wrote a prospectus. We just said, 'We're going into business; would you like to support us?' We had a track record. There was clearly a great demand for semiconductors. It was still a rapid growth environment during that time." This informal, relaxed, laid-back approach not only formed the basic philosophy of their new company, but also persuaded Rock to put together $2 million in seed money for the new corporation, which Noyce and Moore called Intel Corporation.

A year later, they were joined by another defector from Fairchild Semiconductor, Andrew S. Grove, a bearded, dark-haired refugee from the 1956 Hungarian uprising who had worked his way through New York's City College of Engineering and gotten his Ph.D. in chemical engineering from the University of California before joining Noyce and Moore.

This triumvirate had a long-term goal for Intel: to exploit emerging LSI semiconductor technology to its utmost while developing the sort of comfortable, trusting corporate environment in which they wanted to work. They also felt that this new management technique—first proposed by Robert Townsend of Avis and later to be melded into "Theory Y" management principles—would not only attract good scientists and engineers, but encourage them, through self-discipline, to produce new ideas and products well ahead of competitors. They wanted to implement "Management by Objective" (MBO), not just give lip service to it as so many other firms had done (and still do).

Many other companies, including some new ones, were deeply involved in exploiting IC technology and creating electronic circuit modules that would perform tasks formerly done by larger modules built on circuit boards with discrete components. Intel went to work on products specifically for computer applications. In particular, they started development on LSI computer memory modules.

As computers began to find uses in more varied applications, such as airline and hotel reservations or banking, more and more memory was required in which to store data as well as program instructions. IBM had pioneered the magnetic core memory, which depended upon an invention, the magnetic pulse controlling device, developed by the Chinese immigrant scientist Dr. An Wang. (Wang became the founder, chairman, and chief executive officer of Wang Laboratories, which, in 1964, produced the first electronic scientific desk calculators and is still building computers today.) Reel-to-reel tape storage systems were far and away the most ubiquitous and visible computer memories and data storage units. But these were slow in comparison to the earlier vacuum tube and electrostatic memories and in comparison to the transistorized versions of the vacuum tube memory units. Electrostatic memories and vacuum tube memories were *fast* because, if the computer knew where the data was located in such a memory, it could go directly to it. On the other hand, even if the computer knew where the desired data was stored on tape, it had to reel through the tape to that location. It's analogous to the difference between disk recordings and tape recordings for stereo; it's possible to move the stylus arm quickly to that band on the stereo disk containing the music selection desired, whereas reel-to-reel and cassette tapes must be wound past the tape head until the proper location is reached.

It appeared that two different types of memory storage

systems were needed: (a) a fast-access or "random-access" memory like the transistor-based memory unit that the computer could get into and out of fast and that would handle both programming instructions and data being processed but temporarily being stored, and (b) a fast-access memory that was semipermanent like tape.

Intel's first products were the LSI versions of transistor memory boards. In 1970, Intel introduced the first practical dynamic Random Access Memory (RAM).

Ironically, in light of subsequent events, the incentive for Intel to produce the next breakthrough in the computer LSI field came from Japan. In mid-1969, a Japanese desktop calculator manufacturer named Busicom approached Intel with a contract to develop a family of ICs that Busicom could use in a planned line of programmable desk calculators. Assigned to examining the Busicom requirements was Marcian E. "Ted" Hoff, who had joined Intel the year before as its twelfth employee.

After a thorough analysis of the Busicom requirements, Hoff concluded that the proposed Busicom calculator design was far too expensive to be cost-effective in the desk calculator marketplace of the time. He felt that what Busicom wanted wasn't possible with the state of the art and the price structure that Busicom would have to set up to stay in business, even with manufacturing costs in Japan being far lower than in the United States.

But Ted Hoff was also experimenting with one of the first IC computers, the PDP-8 minicomputer made by Digital Equipment Corporation (DEC). A lot of the DEC PDP-8 was made up of encapsulated circuit modules. It therefore had a simple central processing unit that could be easily programmed. Hoff discovered that the DEC minicomputer could do everything that the Busicom chip set would have to do, but it was far simpler. However, the DEC minicomputer was much larger than the proposed Busicom desk calculator. The expensive and difficult feature of the Busicom calculator was its complicated internal logic, its built-in set of operational instructions. On the other hand, the DEC unit had very simple internal logic circuits backed up by a vast memory capability that allowed complex software programs to tell the simple hardware what to do.

Hoff reasoned: why not reduce the built-in complexity and

support a simple central processor with extensive external memory chips such as Intel was already making? Why not put the *entire* central processing unit on a single LSI chip, creating a "computer on a chip"? Then program its operation from software loaded into the external memory chips. Such a simple processor, Hoff believed, could find a wide variety of uses as produced and without any customized internal changes. Instructions for changing its operation to fit specialized applications could be put into and stored in attached memory units.

Noyce, with his extensive background in transistors and ICs, was enthusiastic. The rest of Intel's management was too, because this was a young company seeking new markets. Hoff was given permission to continue the research and development of a chip-based central processing unit or CPU.

The design Hoff came up with required four different chips. One was the microminiaturized central processor, which didn't have a name yet, but later came to be called a "microprocessor." The second was a preprogrammed memory chip, a "read-only memory," or ROM, which would have instructions permanently loaded into it for customized applications and which couldn't be erased or wouldn't have its data disappear when the power was turned off. The third was a "blank slate" memory chip to hold data entered by the user for a given computational operation, a unit that is now called a "Random Access Memory," or RAM, chip. The last of the four was a simple shift register chip to keep track of what data was where and where to send the next data batch.

Intel was able to negotiate with Busicom the right to market the new chip inventions independently, an agreement that the Japanese at Busicom probably grew to regret. In 1970, chip design proceeded under the direction of Dr. Fererico Faggin, who would later leave Intel to start one of Intel's most innovative competitors, Zilog, Inc.

In spite of a management structure that favored and encouraged innovation, the introduction of the first microprocessor chip met with some hesitation on the part of Intel's board of directors. Production and marketing would require a lot of money. In 1969 and 1970, Intel had had a negative cash flow situation and negative net income. Even after Busicom had freed Intel from the exclusivity agreements of their contract, Intel's board of directors couldn't agree on whether or not to proceed with the commerical sale of the microprocessor. The Intel marketing department wasn't encouraging. Amazingly enough, they thought that the microprocessors could be sold only as minicomputer replacements. Intel's marketing people estimated that the entire worldwide market for microprocessors would be only a few thousand units per year!

But the board of directors gave the go-ahead. After all, they had formed Intel because their former employers had seemed unwilling to take risks such as this. In November 1971, Intel introduced the 4004 microprocessor with an ad in *Electronic News*.

The Intel 4004 microprocessor reduced most of the innards of a computer to a large-scale integrated circuit containing twenty-three hundred transistor circuits on a silicon chip approximately a quarter of an inch square. It was a primitive 4-bit processor capable of handling bytes made up of only four binary numbers. But it could be programmed to do *any* computer task and needed only to be supported by an adequate number of RAM chips and input-output devices.

Furthermore, like any IC, it could be manufactured at low cost by the thousands rather than having to be assembled from discrete components and hand-wired like its minicomputer predecessors. It was reliable like an IC. And it was cheap even at several hundred dollars. Because it could be mass produced, the cost came down sharply and rapidly until the price of a micro- processor was less than ten dollars.

No longer did someone have to sit down and design a computer, building it up piece by piece. A complete computer could be bought on a tiny silicon chip.

Technologies alway move forward on two fronts. First is the refinement of the technology. Once a breakthrough has been made and a market created, competitive firms come into the game intent upon capturing a share of the marketplace by refining existing designs, increasing efficiency, and reducing price. The second direction of movement is in advancing the technology, building upon the original foundation to create new technology. Microprocessor technology took both directions in the 1970s.

Even as the 4004 microprocessor was being introduced to market, Intel was working on the 8008 microprocessor. The big difference between the two was that the 8008 was an 8-bit unit.

That meant it could work with numbers made up of eight binary numbers to a word, or byte, rather than merely four. A 4-bit byte can handle decimal numbers up to 32 while an 8-bit byte can take decimal numbers up to 256. A 4-bit processor can handle numbers, but not the ASCII code for the alphabet; whereas an 8-bit byte can handle alpha-numerics. However, the 8008 8-bit microprocessor required twenty additional support chips in contrast to the 4004 with its three additional types.

Competition entered the microprocessor business within a year. As a result, technical refinement was accelerated. By 1974, nineteen different microprocessor products had been announced, followed in 1975 by forty. The year 1976 saw fifty new microprocessors on the market. Each model featured modifications to satisfy specific markets. This worked in both directions, incidentally, because the refinements created new customers who suddenly discovered that the general-purpose microprocessor could be used in their own unique product or manufacturing process where computers had never been used before because of complexity or cost.

The 8-bit microprocessor was quickly followed by the 16-bit processor from National Semiconductor.

RCA developed a microprocessor that would retain its RAM with very low power, allowing batteries to be utilized as stand-by power sources when the machine was turned off or when there was a power failure.

Texas Instruments developed a family of 4-bit microprocessors specifically designed for computer games in the consumer market.

IBM had gotten into IC production in 1964 with their IBM System/360. For this computer system, their Watson Research Center had developed a half-inch ceramic chip on which were deposited and plated various minicomputer circuits. IBM converted the System/360 to monolithic technology with the Model 145 in 1971. By 1978, IBM was mass producing RAM memory chips with a capacity of sixty-four thousand bytes.

By 1974, microprocessor development came full circle back to Hoff's original work as Digital Equipment Corporation introduced a computer that used the Intel 8008 microprocessor.

This accelerated development of LSI technology combined with a rapidly increasing market for a wide variety of microprocessors also pushed hard on quality-control technology. This was and still is one of the major technical problem areas of LSI chip manufacture. Most people have no conception of the length to which quality-control engineers had to take their technology in order to prevent microscopic bits of dirt from getting into the product. Dirt itself came to have a new meaning: any material, no matter how small or in how little concentration or amount, that wasn't wanted in the final product. Simple doping of semiconductor materials requires the ability to introduce impurities on a level of parts per million. Therefore, measurement of such contaminant levels had to be much better than that. Noyce himself remarked: "I used to characterize our business as compared to others in the industry as working on the edge of disaster. . . . It's very, very easy to make a mistake. We're working where a speck of dust ruins everything. . . ."

There were over two hundred distinct and major steps in the production of a single microprocessor chip. Each step had stringent quality-control requirements to prevent dirt from getting into the product. Water used in the manufacturing process had to be superpure, with no more than seventeen parts per *billion* of contaminants present, a feat that was impossible in chemistry a mere twenty years before. Ice cubes made from such superpure water sparkle like diamonds. No dust or dirt particles larger than 1/50,000th of an inch could be present in concentrations of more than a hundred per cubic foot of air. For comparison, that's a thousandth of what's permitted in an ordinary hospital's operating room. Lead pencils couldn't be used because the dust that's a residue from their marks on paper could ruin the production process. Indeed, even diskettes and data record tapes used with home computers, shouldn't have their labels marked using lead pencils because of the possibility of minute quantities of microscopic carbon particles getting from the mark to the recording surface.

Although the microprocessor was hailed as the electronic product of the decade, it was far from reaching its full potential as a device that would add "intelligence" to machines and instruments. A step toward that was made with the Intel 8080 microprocessor. This was developed by Masatoshi Shima, who later designed the Z-80 microprocessor for Zilog, Inc., before returning to Japan to head the Intel Design Center there. The 8080 was ten times faster than the 8008 and had a memory of 64,000 bytes (64K memory). It required only six additional support chips in contrast to the twenty required by the 8008. It also had the capability to control external devices.

The response to the 8080 was enormous, making it the most popular *and* the most imitated microprocessor of the time. This led to the development of two important and valuable competitive products. The Motorola 6800 was one and required only a single power supply in contrast to the multiple supplies required by previous microprocessors. The Motorola 6800 also came to the market supported by a wide range of peripherals circuit chips that improved its usefulness. Another microprocessor, the Zilog Z-80, appeared in 1976 and featured two years of improvements over the original Intel 8080.

These three microprocessors—the Intel 8080, the Motorola 6800, and the Zilog Z-80—opened up new markets that had never before considered electronics or computers useful.

But the people at Intel weren't satisfied with the success of the 8008 and 8080. In a young company such as Intel, it's easy to compound success once you get going, provided management continues to support technological innovation and progress. By the time Zilog brought out the Z-80, Intel was ready to introduce the 8048, which was the actual computer on a chip, a single chip containing a microcomputer that incorporated all the diverse functions formerly handled by supporting chips—processing, input/output, and both ROM and RAM.

It took only three years for the total number of microprocessors in use to exceed the entire number of minicomputers and large main-frame computers then in use. The microprocessor market had grown from nothing to $3.7 million per year, nearly tripling in size every year!

None of this microprocessor technology or hardware would have been more than a nifty laboratory trick if it hadn't also been for parallel developments in the technology of fast, dense recording and recall of data from storage as well as technology capable of displaying and printing quickly and accurately the enormous flood of data that could be handled by the fast microprocessors. Whether the microprocessor chip drove the other technologies or those technologies were self-perpetuating is unknown. Perhaps they drove each other.

Intel had started by developing a RAM chip. Others followed. The technology of RAM and ROM memory chips was

well established by the mid-1970s. The time it took a microprocessor to find the data it needed in a RAM or ROM, the "access
time," dropped to about 250 nanoseconds (a nanosecond is a
billionth of a second). Reliability had increased to the point
where only 0.009 percent of all memory chips could be expected
to fail after a thousand hours of operation. To provide some
perspective and comparison, if this same sort of reliability could
be achieved in the automotive industry, only *ninety* out of each
million automobiles produced each model year would require
any sort of repair at all.

Long-term semipermanent memory storage development
was required in order to come up with a fast and reliable
replacement for tape units. This itself came out of progress in
tape recording technology, based in turn on thin-film technology. And it required engineers to make a synthesis between
reel-to-reel tape recording and disk recording.

Ordinary stereo disks use the same technology invented in
1877 by Thomas Alva Edison for the very first phonograph,
called his "only original invention." A groove is cut by a stylus
into a solid base; this groove has varying width and depth, with
frequency and displacement equal to the frequency and ampli-
tude of the recorded sound; during playback, the mechanical
movement of the pickup stylus is converted back into electronic
signals, which are then converted into sound.

But the recording of electrical signals by electromagnetic
means on a flexible plastic tape coated with iron oxide had made
enormous strides since the German firm, Telefunken, came up
with the first such reel-to-reel system (which became part of the
war booty in 1945).

Magnetic tape technology has made enormous technical
progress since then. In 1953, the best available technology
permitted 100 bits per linear inch of tape and a read-write speed
of 7,500 bits per second. By 1966, this had risen to 1,600 bits per
inch and 180,000 bits per second. In 1983, it was 6,250 bits per
inch and 1,250,000 bits per second. Part of this progress came
from requirements in video recording, but part of it was also
driven by computer technology. This is a case where the requirements of two different areas produced results useful to
both probably in less time than if the technology had had only
one driver.

When this tape recording technology was combined with the rotating disk, IBM engineers created a compact information storage system that combined the features of the disk's fast access by a recording head with the semipermanent high-density features of tape recording. The memory disk was born.

The first such data disk was, surprisingly enough, the "floppy," or flexible, disk introduced by IBM in 1971. The 8-inch-diameter floppy bred its cousin, the smaller 5¼-inch "minifloppy." Both could store enormous amounts of data. By 1978, the minifloppy could store as much as 630K 8-bit bytes on its surface. IBM pushed the read-write rates as high as 1,250,000 bits per second. In 1973, IBM introduced the 3340 disk unit, which has become known universally as the "Winchester" disk because this was IBM's internal development code name for it. The original 3340 Winchester disk unit featured a ski-shaped recording head that rode on a layer of air 18 millionths of an inch thick. The recording density of this 1973 development was 1.7 million bits per square inch. Naturally, it's improved since then.

Other magnetic data storage systems were perfected, although the floppy, minifloppy, and three-inch microfloppy are by far the most ubiquitous today. The magnetically encoded tape strip on the back of credit cards came from identical tape strips used in 1970 computers for inserting program data.

LSI and magnetic recording technologies developed in the 1970s allowed computers to become very small and fast with extremely large working and storage memories. But there was and still is a problem getting data into and out of computers as fast as they can process and produce it.

Early computers used ordinary teletypewriters and teleprinters working at about one hundred words per minute. A teletype machine is an incredible collection of mechanical buffoonery that will tear itself to pieces if left unattended for long periods of time. It had one saving grace for the early computer period: teletypewriters were relatively cheap because they could be obtained from government surplus. Eventually, however, computer engineers had to do something because the teletypewriters were so *slow*.

All sorts of fascinating Victorian technical approaches have been taken in an attempt to speed up the printing of computer output. The IBM Selectric and other electric typewriters were adapted. To speed up the sort of "letter quality" printing that these slow electric typewriters could produce, the "daisy wheel" and NCR Spinwriter printers were developed; they can handle up to one thousand words per minute. "Dot matrix" printers, which were faster, were developed. Ink-jet printers were faster yet.

In 1979, IBM applied laser technology to printers and came up with the IBM 3800, which could print twenty thousand *lines* per minute. In 1982, the IBM 3800 was given greater resolution by the use of a split-beam laser whose beam was altered millions of times per second by being reflected from an eighteen-sided mirror spinning at twelve thousand revolutions per minute. This was as much a step forward as the ENIAC was over the electromechanical punch-card machines and may signal the beginning of something just as significant: the use of submicroscopic electrons and photons in place of relatively massive mechanical moving parts in printers.

The 1970s saw astounding progress in computer technology. Some of the applications of this technology and the consequences thereof weren't foreseen, but developed right along with it.

15

Computer in Your Pocket

The invention of the microprocessor in 1971 set the stage for what might be termed the "personalization" of computers. Up to that time, the size, complexity, cost, and programming difficulties of computers had limited their use to large government, business, financial, and academic institutions. The microprocessor, coupled with other LSI developments, immediately dropped the size, complexity, and cost factors by orders of magnitude, opening the potential market to an entirely new type of consumer.

Some people saw this immediately and established new companies to rush into the perceived new markets.

Others, who had been in the electronics business for a long time, also saw it and managed to take their established firms into the new markets in a massive diversification.

Quite contrary to what might have been expected, the first products that emerged were not small versions of the large main-frame computers, but a step beyond: the pocket calculator. It was as though the computer industry jumped from first base to third, then later came back and touched second.

In a way, the people who made this unusual move might have been extremely shrewd marketeers, because once one managed to get one's hands on a pocket calculator made with the new LSI technology, the way was paved for this person to move on to a personal microcomputer.

First of all, a calculator is a highly specialized and limited class of computer. It's designed and intended to carry out arithmetic and other mathematical operations. The input is usually from an integral keyboard. Output is either some sort of numerical display on the machine or a printed paper tape. The first Burroughs adding machines were calculators. So were the NCR cash registers, and the Monroe, Marchant, and Friden desk calculators of various types that followed, as well as most desk adding machines. So a calculator isn't a full-blown general-purpose computer. Some companies lost sight of this.

The pocket calculator is actually a modernized electronic digital version of the classic calculators, the Oriental abacus and the Napier slide rule.

Two engineers saw this immediately.

One of them is William R. Hewlett. Born in 1913 while his father, Dr. A. W. Hewlett, was at the University of Michigan, Bill Hewlett grew up in the academic environment of Stanford University, where his father came to teach at the medical school. He got his A.B. degree at Stanford in 1934, where he came to know a classmate, David Packard, a native of Pueblo, Colorado, who got his A.B. degree the same year. During their undergraduate years at Stanford, the two men became very close friends. They liked to go on long backpacking trips together in the Colorado Rockies.

Professor Frederick E. Terman, who'd set up the Stanford Electronics Research Laboratory, became their mentor. At Terman's urging, Hewlett and Packard visited Philo Farnsworth and other early electronics entrepreneurs who were developing radio and television gear in the free enterprise arena around San Francisco. As David Packard later recalled: "I was very intrigued to see what these people were doing. And it was really as a result of these visits, and discussion with Fred Terman and Bill Hewlett toward the latter half of my senior year, that we decided that maybe we'd try and make a run for it ourselves."

But it didn't happen right away. Although they'd talked seriously about setting up their own business, it was the middle of the Great Depression. Packard got a job offer from General Electric in early 1934, and even though it paid him less than a dollar an hour, he couldn't turn it down because jobs for engineers weren't plentiful then. So he went east to work on vacuum tubes, specifically high-current AC-rectifying "ignitron" tubes, at General Electric's facility in Schenectady, New York.

Hewlett stayed in Palo Alto for a year after graduation, went back to MIT to get an M.S. in 1936, then returned to Stanford to do some electrical research and to get an electrical engineering degree from Stanford under Terman's guidance. He built diathermy machines for local medical clinics and a bulky electroencephalograph (EEG) for a doctor at Stanford Medical School. He had to prepare a thesis to meet the requirements for his electrical engineering degree, so his thesis adviser, Professer Terman, did what most thesis advisers do to graduate students: steer their thesis work toward some problem that interests the thesis adviser, especially if the student has no strong interest in specific research problems. Terman suggested Hewlett look into some of the possibilities of the then-new concept of "negative feedback."

General Radio, one of the pioneering firms in the wireless industry, had designed a fixed-frequency audio oscillator as a test instrument. It used a combination of fixed resistors and capacitors to generate discrete audio frequencies, and these predetermined frequencies could be selected by push buttons on its front panel. It was one of the first audio oscillators and was used to test the audio circuits of radio broadcast facilities. Terman thought this was an instrument of restricted usefulness, especially in research, because of the limited number of preset frequencies it could generate. He thought that an audio oscillator could be built utilizing negative feedback principles that would produce a continuously variable frequency. So he suggested to Hewlett: "Here's an idea. Maybe you can develop it into something useful."

Bill Hewlett worked out the details and the design, then built a nicely packaged prototype. He'd developed some unique new circuits, and the audio oscillator was a patentable device as a result. It also looked like the sort of thing that could be a good initial product for a small company, and Hewlett remembered that he and Packard had had long discussions about just such a possibility when the right device came along. The audio oscillator could be it. But Packard was on the East Coast with GE, where he was making a name for himself in the design of special vacuum tubes. It looked like it would be very difficult to entice Packard back to Palo Alto.

Then, through an unusual chain of circumstances, Terman's Stanford Electronics Research Laboratory received a $1,000 grant—big money for those depression days—from the Sperry Gyroscope Company, later to become Sperry Rand, makers of the UNIVAC computer. Then as now, some university professors have such an outstanding reputation and such good contacts that they can manage to arrange funding for interesting projects in interesting ways. Sperry wanted to have Terman's laboratory do some development work improving a microwave radar tube called a klystron (now used in microwave ovens) developed by another Palo Alto duo, the brothers Sigurd and Russell Varian. Because of Packard's expertise in vacuum tubes, which he'd picked up with GE, Terman thought he'd be ideal for this work. So he asked Hewlett: "Do you think Dave would be interested in taking a leave of absence from GE to work on this project for nine months or so? We could pay him $55 a month for nine months, and still have $500 for expenses."

Hewlett wrote Packard with the proposition, and Packard took a leave of absence from GE to return to Palo Alto. The people at GE were very puzzled; they couldn't understand why Packard wanted to break his continuity as a very successful vacuum tube engineer just to go back to Stanford.

Back in Palo Alto, Packard worked part time on the klystron tube project and the remainder of his time on formal courses leading to his electrical engineering degree under Terman in 1939. But he knew within a few weeks that he'd never return to GE because of Hewlett's audio oscillator.

Together, Bill Hewlett and Dave Packard formed the partnership Hewlett-Packard in 1939. Their only product was the oscillator, which they called the "Hewlett-Packard Model 200A." They chose the designation because "the number sounded big." Terman arranged a deal with ITT that paid for getting a patent on Bill's oscillator, in return for which ITT got some rights for it. Hewlett and Packard didn't have enough money to get a patent themselves.

In 1940, Packard took the prototype to the national electronics show and convention sponsored in those days by the Institute for Radio Engineers (IRE). The entire exhibit was held in the ballroom of the Commodore Hotel in New York City. They started to sell them, one at a time, and they didn't make one until they had an order in house for it. That meant they could get the money to buy the parts to make it. They made their audio oscillators in Dave Packard's garage and sold them for $55 each against competitive equipment that cost anywhere from $200 to $600.

"Bill found this house on Addison Avenue in Palo Alto," Packard remembered. "The house is still there, as a matter of fact. We rented the lower floor, where my wife Lu and I lived. There was a little building out back where Bill lived, and a garage that we set up as a shop to work in."

Terman recalls that he could tell when the fledgling firm had received a new order. "If Dave Packard's car was parked in the garage, there was no backlog. But if the car was parked in the driveway, business was good."

Then H-P got their first big sale. The sound engineer for Walt Disney's motion picture *Fantasia* saw the oscillator and recognized what it could do for checking out the complex audio system for the movie's musical effects. *Fantasia* was the first motion picture with multiple sound tracks (what we call "stereo" today). Disney wanted a different physical configuration and a different audio-frequency range, so the Hewlett-Packard Audio Oscillator Model 200B was born shortly thereafter. Disney bought eight of them at one crack. One of them reportedly is still operating at the Walt Disney Studios in Burbank.

The Hewlett-Packard Model 200 Audio Oscillator was its own best salesman. It had greater capabilities than any competitive product and was priced several hundred dollars less than any of them.

In 1940, the company had outgrown the garage and moved into a small building nearby. By 1942, H-P had to construct their own building. The partnership of the two men worked well, each one complementing the other. Dave Packard recalled: "Bill, I think, has been a little more interested in the engineering side and I was more interested in the business side."

Their next product was a vacuum tube voltmeter, followed by other electrical measuring instruments. Within a short period of time, Hewlett-Packard became one of the world's leading manufacturers of electronic test equipment, instruments that are used in the laboratory and even on the production line to measure the performance of equipment as it is being designed, manufactured, operated, or serviced. Because of Bill Hewlett's early interest and work in medical electronics—he had built diathermy machines and EEGs for Palo Alto and Stanford medical clinics—H-P also continued to expand in this field with equipment for patient monitoring, diagnosis, and therapy. This took the firm into the areas of analytical instruments to determine and measure the chemical components of pharmaceuticals, blood, and other biologicals. In turn, the H-P equipment began to show up in chemical labs, food industries, energy industries, and finally environmental measurement labs.

Bill Hewlett served in the Army during World War II, while Dave Packard stayed in Palo Alto to manage the business. Wartime contracts and production weren't allowed to disrupt R&D, which led the company into the microwave measuring field with a postwar microwave signal generator introduced in 1946.

By 1950, H-P had two hundred employees, seventy products, and $2 million in sales. In 1952, Bill Hewlett and David Packard donated a huge new wing to Terman's Stanford Electronics Research Laboratory.

Hewlett-Packard first got into computers in 1966 not as an addition to their product line, but as a means to check out and improve their own measurement instruments. But it ended up doing much more than that in the years that followed because it changed the meaning of electronic instrumentation to include the computation and analysis of the measured quantities as well as the control of automated measurements. By the mid-1960s, H-P was manufacturing electronic instruments capable of producing measurement data faster and in greater quantities than it could be gathered and analyzed by human beings. The in-house computer they'd built for their own purpose gave birth to another H-P product. In 1966, the company introduced its first computer, designed specifically to work with H-P instruments. In fact, it was called an "instrumentation computer."

This new venture into computers plus the knowledge that Robert Noyce and Ted Hoff had developed in the microprocessor at Intel just down the road in Santa Clara led Hewlett-Packard to the one single product that forever changed the whole image of the computer industry. Although any company could have done it—all the elements were there and the market was ready—Hewlett-Packard was the company that got to market first.

In 1972, Hewlett-Packard startled the world by introducing the HP-35, the first scientific hand-held calculator. It had immediate worldwide impact because it combined the technology of LSI and microprocessor chips with Light Emitting Diode (LED) numeric displays, a comparatively large (for its time) internal memory of several registers, and battery or AC operation. And it was lightweight, small in size, easy to program, and "user friendly." Even though its operating system required the use of a strange inverted manner of entering data called RPN for "Reverse Polish Notation" (not an ethnic computer joke, but the notation for the way computers handle sequences of arithmetic operations; it derives from Boolean algebra), it had immediate worldwide impact. Within only a few years, it made the old slide rule obsolete.

There were problems involved with its acceptance, however. Many old-fashioned academicians and schoolteachers thought that the HP-35 made life too easy for students because it could handle trig functions, logarithms, reciprocals, exponentials, roots, factorials, natural logs, hyperbolic functions, and most other straightforward mathematical operations that the profs when *they* were students had to look up in huge tables. So they expected their 1970s students to do the same. Not a chance. Not only did the HP-35 make many homework problems mere matters of pushing the proper buttons in the proper sequence on an HP-35, but the answers were usually right as well.

Nearly everyone today remembers getting their first simple four-function (addition, subtraction, multiplication, and division) hand calculator. The demand was enormous in 1972 and 1973. Although many people couldn't afford several hundred dollars for an HP-35, they could buy a simple four-function unit such as the one made by American Circuitron, Inc., of Hamden, Connecticut (one of the hundreds of little pocket calculator companies that sprang up in those years to fill the huge market desire for pocket calculators) for $100. Today, a calculator that does the same things and more can be purchased for less than $10 and is the size of a wristwatch. With LSI microprocessor chips and other parts coming off the assembly lines, it became very easy to make a pocket calculator. The computer chip was available along with the keyboard, the LED display, and the nickle-cadmium batteries and AC charger. Unlike the HP-35, with its Reverse Polish Notation, most other calculators operated with normal algebraic entry—key 5, key +, key 6, key =. So have most pocket calculators since that time.

Texas Instruments, Inc., of Dallas was and still is one of the strongest competitors in the pocket calculator field. TI followed H-P into the marketplace in 1973 with the Texas Instruments SR-50 Slide Rule Calculator and a host of other pocket calculators designed for specific applications such as finance and business. The SR-50 gave the HP-35 a run for its money. About the same size and weight as the HP-35 (which set the standards in those areas), the SR-50 had a ni-cad battery pack with AC charger and an LED display. It calculated to thirteen significant figures and displayed answers rounded off to ten significant digits. From keyboard entry it would perform simple arithmetic, reciprocals, exponentiation, roots, trigonometric, hyperbolic, and logarithmic functions, all in full floating decimal point or in scientific notation. It had three working registers and one storage register. Except for large factorials, it would complete a calculation in less than a tenth of a second. It sold for about $75, well under the HP-35's price.

TI got into the pocket calculator market in a big way, producing hundreds of different models in different price ranges with different capabilities. Texas Instruments' designers and engineers got to be very good with calculator technology, so good in fact that it caused them difficulty later on.

The technology of pocket calculators bred some interesting offspring, too. At the heart of every central processing unit or microprocessor in every computer is a clock that beats time for the computer and provides the time base for turning units on and off in order to shunt data around to the proper places in the computer in the proper sequences according to the program instructions. This computer clock is an electronic oscillator controlled by a quartz crystal just as similar equipment controls the broadcasting frequency of AM, FM, and television stations as well as CB radio gear. Normally, this timing circuit or clock runs at a frequency of two to four million cycles per second (megaHertz or, abbreviated, mHz). The crystal that locks the frequency may be running at another frequency, and transistorized integrated circuits may be multiplying it up or dividing it down to the desired timing frequency. In small computers like pocket calculators, the higher the basic clock frequency, the smaller the crystal can be, since its natural frequency is a function of its dimensions.

Engineers at Texas Instruments asked themselves the question: "Why not just take the timing circuitry out of the pocket calculator and turn it into a superaccurate digital wrist-watch?"

It was a natural spin-off product because all of the technology was there. The quartz crystal oscillator could be made to run at 32,768 pulses per second (Hz). A simple LSI chip can be easily designed to divide this oscillator frequency in half fifteen times to create one pulse every second. This division register can be tapped at suitable places to produce pulses at a rate of both ten and a hundred per second.

The first digital watches used LED displays requiring a relatively large amount of battery power, thus necessitating large watch batteries that had to be replaced often. In 1974, "liquid crystal" technology made its appearance. Liquid crystals are microscopic in size and some liquid crystal substances can have these microscopic elements aligned by the application of an electric field. Once aligned in opposition to a polarizing surface film, they show up as a dark mark against a mirrored surface. Since liquid crystal displays require far less power, they need smaller batteries.

Minor modifications in the structure of the controlling microprocessor chip in the digital watch can permit it to have other features such as stopwatch capabilities with lap times, countdown stopwatch ability, multiple time zone readouts, and day-and-date calendars.

The first TI digital watches were expensive in comparison to their major competition: battery-powered analog watches, some of them quartz crystal controlled for highest accuracy. But, by 1984, a simple digital clock module complete with battery, liquid crystal read-out, and calendar was retailing for $4.95 *or less*. Considering that the "standard" mark-up on most products is five times the cost of labor and materials, this means that such a miracle of electronics costs less than a dollar at the shipping dock.

The inexpensive digital watch practically ruined the traditional clock and watch companies such as Bulova and Longines-Wittnauer. The Accutron crystal-controlled electric watch, pride of the 1960s, practically disappeared. U.S. Time, makers of Westclox, found themselves in real trouble. Timex, long-time makers of inexpensive mechanical analog watches and clocks, did a quick change-over into the digital watch business and managed to survive.

But in order to meet price competition, nearly all digital watches today are made in the Orient. Digital watches, along with pocket calculators, created one of the biggest eras of technological transfer and export ever seen as U.S. companies rushed to establish overseas factories where labor costs were lower. They had to take the technology with them to the Orient. The Japanese, never very far behind in high technology, were also there and waiting. Today, nearly every digital watch is made in Taiwan, Hong Kong, or other low-cost labor centers in the Far East. And most digital watches bear the names of Oriental manufacturers.

The same rush eastward was made by the pocket calculator manufacturers, and they met the Japanese on the same grounds with the same ideas. Canon, Sharp, Casio—these are but a few of the names that appear on both digital watches and pocket calculators today. True, you can still buy the great-great-great-grandson of the HP-35 or the TI SR-50, but chances are it costs less because it was made in Taiwan.

In the late 1970s, pocket calculators and digital watches got together again to produce the wrist calculator-watch. The most popular of these was the Casio C-800 model, which combined a digital clock, day-date calendar, stopwatch, dual time zone clock, and four-function push-button calculator. In 1983, the calculator keys disappeared from the front of this watch; the Casio TC-800 operates by simply touching the coated glass watch cover, making use of body capacitance to complete the contact.

The computer on a chip had become the computer in the wristwatch. In the next decade, that wristwatch probably will be able to talk to a satellite.

16

The Computer Becomes Personal

$\mathbb{B}$y 1975, computer technology had advanced on all fronts. A host of new companies had entered the industry. But the Big Boys who made both complete computer systems and computer components still included IBM, Intel, Digital Equipment Corporation, Burroughs, NCR, Honeywell, Motorola, Control Data Corporation, and Hewlett-Packard. Big computers got smaller in size and more powerful in their abilities to process large amounts of data faster.

Many businesses had been lured into the pioneering task of computerizing or automating their offices or factories in the late 1960s, leading to the first big computer bust. Programming was still in a relatively primitive state, a factor that contributed to the disaffection. First, the computers were large and expensive. Second, they were difficult to operate, making it easier in many cases to keep the clerks and bookkeepers on the payroll. And last, the companies that tried to computerize really didn't understand their own systems or procedures. As a result, computerization turned out to be a very expensive experiment that didn't work.

One Wall Street securities analyst was reported to have remaked in 1971: "The computer has just about had it."

But the computerized companies as well as the computer

manufacturers did have to hire a lot of computer programmers, leading to an expansion in the programmer employment field, which in turn drew in many young people who discovered that programming wasn't as much technical as it was a way of thinking. These young people, many of them from the "flower children" generation of the 1960s, discovered something that was really all their own: programming. And it became their profession as well as their hobby. This was a critical factor in what was about to happen.

Nobody guessed that there were enormous new computer markets "out there" just waiting for the proper hardware and software.

Two such markets were for small business computers and personal or "home" computers.

The development of the microprocessor, advances in memory technology, new means for a computer to communicate with humans, and new programs to make computers "user friendly" did not produce the personal computer. The needs of commerical business did. In turn, the personal computer evolved from the small business computer in the late 1970s because of the computer buffs.

No established computer company believed in 1975 that there was any market for a personal computer. But, typically, the marketing forecasts and estimates were wrong.

It was difficult to see that the youngsters who'd grown up with computers and lived with computers every day wanted their own computers. These computer buffs were usually far down the corporate ladder where most of the older managers and executives didn't pay much attention to them. They were also relatively few then. It was only when computer buffs grew in numbers and began to want their own computers that the mere possibility of the existence of a personal computer market began slowly to dawn upon the marketing managers who advised the computer executives. What we call today the computer "hackers" created the first personal computers.

In the meantime, the business computer industry backed off, tried to discover what it had been doing wrong, and attempted to take off in new directions.

It was decided that business computers had to be smaller. The computers had to be able to directly solve the most urgent business problems, primarily those in the office. If a number of small computers could be used, they could also be linked together or "networked" to talk to one another if necessary, thereby eliminating the need for a big general-purpose mainframe computer that operated in a time-sharing mode with a retinue of remote terminals.

Wang Laboratories established a fine reputation and good profitability in the 1950s and 1960s building electronic counters, machine tool controls, block-tape readers, and encoders. The experience in these fields led Wang to attempt to computerize what now seems to be an obvious target industry for computerization: typesetting. In 1962, Wang Laboratories, Inc., produced the LINASEC, the first electronic justifying typesetter system. By 1964, Wang was producing the Cadillac of the early desktop computers, the LOCI, which foretold the need for a smaller and less powerful computer than the big mainframe units. By 1969, the Wang typesetters and desk calculators had become industry standards. But Dr. Wang, who was very much in charge of his company and called the shots, saw that the LSI chip and other developments would drastically change the marketplace. So he parlayed his company's expertise in typesetting and desk calculators into two major new product areas: office data processing and word processing.

Until Dr. An Wang and his Wang Laboratory people got busy on the word-processing application of the computer, nobody had even guessed that a computer could be used for such a purpose. Actually, a computer word processor, as it developed over the next six years, became more than just a supertypewriter. With the ASCII alpha-numeric code becoming more or less standard among computers, and with the proper programming, a secretary could input the working or RAM memory of a small computer directly from a typewriterlike keyboard laid out in the standard "qwerty" format and then add codes for such things as paragraph endings, program the machine to print out in various formats of line spacing, line width, and page lengths along with page numbers, headers, footers, and right and/or left margin justifications. The word-processing program could also allow storage of the typewritten material on tape or disk.

With a computer-based word processor, no longer would a typist have to retype an entire letter, report, or manuscript. The text could be retrieved from the tape or disk file, corrected on the screen and in the working memory, and either stored in updated form on tape or disk or printed out. Furthermore, a word processor is about four to five times as fast as a typewriter, depending upon the typist's skill. Two of the most important time-saving factors are the elimination of both the need for a carriage return while typing and the need to put a clean sheet of paper in the typewriter at the beginning of every new page.

The first Wang 1200 word processor, intended for office secretarial use, was introduced in 1971 and featured dual tape cassettes, automatic centering of headings, right margin justification, exact column alignment, word search, and other features. In 1976, responding to competition and exploting new programming, memory, and printout technology, the Wang WPS word processor used a cathode-ray tube (CRT) display, featured disk storage of up to four thousand pages of typed material, and worked into a 350-word-per-minute letter-quality printer.

The first of the Wang small business computers, the 2200 series, came on the market in 1972. But Wang's biggest impact was with its word processors. By 1978, Wang was the largest worldwide supplier of CRT word processing systems, with over fifty thousand users and an installed base of $550 million.

IBM didn't and couldn't ignore this. Back in 1933, they'd acquired Electromatic Typewriters, Inc., of Rochester, New York, and were a major office typewriter company by 1949, when they announced the IBM Model A "Executive" Electric Typewriter with proportional spacing. By 1958, IBM alone had sold more than a million electric typewriters. The IBM Selectric typewriter with its type ball and stationary carriage came out in 1961, and this machine not only allowed typists to increase speed, but also could be easily modified to create a letter-quality computer printer. The 1969 IBM "Mag Card" Selectric was a crude and limited word processor, but by 1973 the Mag Card II Typewriter would allow secretaries to magnetically store for later recall the text of a letter as "boilerplate" for multiple letters to different people. But the first IBM product carrying the name "word processor" didn't appear until 1976.

The year 1976 also saw another old-line office equipment company enter the computer-based word-processing field. Lanier Business Products began in Nashville, Tennessee, as the Lanier Company, distributors of Ediphone office dictation equipment. Formed by Tommy, Hicks, and Sartain Lanier, it was strictly a rep and distribution company until it began to diversify in 1942. Lanier became an office dictation equipment manufacturer after changing its name to Lanier Business Products and introducing its own dictation system, the Teletran. The Lanier Text Editor 90 was, in 1976, the second microprocessor-based CRT-screen word processor. Lanier's aggressive newspaper and television advertising campaigns brought to the businessman's (and also the professional author's) attention the potential of the word processor.

But both the Wang and the Lanier systems were expensive—$12,000 and up. This was a price that a mid-size business could afford, but not most professional offices or authors. But by 1976, the computer-based word processor had arrived on the scene, albeit expensively, for those who dealt daily with the typed word.

Progress in the field of the small business computer followed a similar path. Once Wang Laboratories identified a solution to computerizing the business office, other companies followed—NCR, Burroughs, Control Data Corporation, Digital Equipment Corporation, and Hewlett-Packard.

Both the word-processor market and the small business computer market produced two basic approaches to this mini-computerization of the workplace. Two different systems were developed almost parallel to one another.

One was the individual computer-based office machine intended for use by a single individual and with a single terminal, microcomputer, data storage subsystem, and printer. This became known as the "stand-alone" system because it quite literally could stand alone on its own without any external connection except an electric power cord that plugged into the wall.

The second was the multistation small business system, which had two or more individual terminals connected to a single computer, each terminal working with the central main frame on a time-sharing basis. The architecture of such centralized systems could be varied according to business needs. Furthermore, the arrangement could be changed or expanded as the office requirements changed. Sometimes each terminal had its own data storage peripheral in the form of disk or tape storage. It could also have its own printer. Other systems had all storage in the same location as the main frame of the computer.

There were advantages and disadvantages to both types of systems. A system of stand-alones was often more expensive than a centralized system, depending upon how many work station terminals an office required. If few work stations were required, the centralized systems were more expensive. There was a trade-off point in costs between stand-alones and centralized systems, depending upon individual needs and requirements. When a stand-alone goes down and needs repairs to get it back on line, the other stand-alones are not affected; in a centralized system, if some portions of the system go off-line, the whole office system can go down.

There was and still is a major dichotomy in the word processor and business computer situation. A "dedicated" word processor such as the early Wang or the Lanier is just that: dedicated to the word-processing task. At the heart of each of these systems is a microcomputer, but it has been permanently programmed for nothing but word processing. On the other hand, the ordinary, general-purpose microcomputer can be programmed to do many tasks—general accounting, inventory control, scientific and engineering calculations, mailing lists, general data base, filing, *and* word processing. The dedicated word processor may or may not be easier to use; at first it was, but the later development of word-processing programs such as "Electric Pencil" and "WordStar" are just as easy to use in a general-purpose computer. In 1976, the dedicated word processor was perhaps a bit less costly than a general-purpose business computer, but this price spread disappeared in the next five years. Today, dedicated word processors are primarily used where nothing but secretarial-type work is done and where additional computer capability isn't necessary.

By 1975-76, the business office use of computers had defined the microcomputer in matters of size, capability, memory size, speed, and configuration. The prices, however, were high, even though the cost of an individual microprocessor chip had dropped to less than $100.

Before 1975, only about three thousand desktop business computers had been sold. The number of word processors out in the field wasn't much more than that. The price barrier— $12,000 and up for any machine with enough power to be useful for anything more than playing simple games—was formidable. It was holding back an enormous market. Somebody had to break through.

It was the computer buffs, not the big companies, who did so.

The computer buff is an interesting, fascinating, and often inexplicable personality. It's grossly unfair to make a generalization about this sort of person because there are so many different types. Basically, however, the computer buff isn't a new phenomenon. Every time a new technology has come along (and this is especially true in the twentieth century, when technology has provided enough free time and extra money to permit people to have hobbies) it has created its own following of amateurs. The word *amateur* itself contains the key to the phenomenon. It comes from the Italian verb *amator*, "to love." An amateur is a lover of an activity who engages in it simply because of his or her own interest.

Nearly all scientists in the nineteenth century and before were amateurs; they were either independently wealthy or they made their living at some other mundane work. Most of the great advances in both science and technology were made in the nineteenth and early twentieth centuries by amateurs. The Wrights, professional bicycle mechanics, were amateur aviators, for example. Thomas Alva Edison was an amateur who rapidly became the first industrial engineer, although he'd had only a few *months* of formal schooling. The budding technologies of the twentieth century created in their wake hordes of amateurs, some of whom went on to make major contributions to their hobbies.

The phenomenon of the technical hobbyist isn't unique to the computer industry. However, the computer buffs and hackers *do* believe they're unique. They believe that, having always had computers around them for as long as they can remember, they are the first computerized generation. Thus they think and act differently from those technical hobbyists and amateurs who came before them. (Each generation of amateurs has to be different from those preceding it if only because their technology is different, thereby permitting them to do things that would have been impossible for their predecessors.)

The computer buff, like the radio ham, got interested in computers after reading about them in books and magazines or living with them in the workplace, where they were forced to learn something about them in order to get along with them. The computer buff also wanted to have his or her own computer or to get access to one that was faster, more powerful, or simply the latest example of the state of the art.

But even the smallest business computer cost far more than a computer buff could afford.

Cost has never stopped technical amateurs in the past, and it didn't stop the computer buffs. The solution to the cost problem was the same as it has always been.

If you can't buy one, build one.

And even if you can buy one, it's more fun and a little cheaper to build your own and end up with a lot more performance for the dollar.

Slowly but surely, individual computer buffs began to know one another. The contacts came accidentally, as a result of friends, or as a result of that strange new computer phenomenon, the computer network "bulletin board." This latter was available only to those who had access to a computer or who had developed their own, had gotten access to a computer network in which many computers were tied together with a big computer via telephone lines, and had left or found messages about computer clubs on the inevitable bulletin board memory space that came to be established on every computer net.

Computer parts slowly began to become available in both electronic parts stores and in the electronic junk yards that spring up around every high-technology center.

The first personal computer product shows were offshoots of the swap nights of local computer clubs where everyone would bring their unwanted or surplus computer boards and other hardware. Soon, people were developing and building specialized hardware, bringing it to club meetings, and swapping or selling it.

Enterprising computer buffs suddenly became aware of market forces and the desires of their fellow buffs for keypads, memory boards, CPU boards, and all the other elements of small computers.

It occurred to some of them that personal computer kits might sell.

This is exactly and precisely the way it happened fifty years and twenty-five years earlier with the radio hams and hi-fi enthusiasts, respectively. The computer buffs were no different. Only the technology and the products were different.

Two of these young entrepreneurs were to parlay this phenomenon into the first of the successful personal computer companies.

In early 1976, two self-made engineers, Steven P. Jobs (then twenty-one) and Stephen G. Wozniak (then twenty-six), collaborated on the design of a specialized computer plug-in board for the growing number of home-built personal computers on-line in the Santa Clara Valley of California, the breeding ground for new high-tech activities for over fifty years. They decided to expand it into a full-fledged personal computer kit. It took them six months to design the prototype and forty hours to build it. Almost immediately, they got fifty orders for their personal computer kit.

But it would take capital to set up their company. So they raised $1,350 by selling Jobs's used Volkswagen van and a programmable pocket calculator. Following tradition—although they may not have realized it at the time and might have objected to the idea that they were in the grand tradition of De Forest, Farnsworth, Hewlett, Packard, Noyce, and their predecessors—they set up business in Jobs's garage.

They named their computer and their company "Apple" because to them the apple represented the simplicity they were trying to achieve in the design and use of a personal computer.

The first Apple computer kit was so successful that the orders flowed in faster than Jobs and Wozniak could ship kits out the garage door. Their success also showed them that they were undercapitalized. But, unlike Hewlett and Packard, Jobs and Wozniak were not a team balanced between technology and business acumen; they were both computer buffs. They decided to hire a professional manager.

Through a mutual friend, they found A. C. "Mike" Markkula, Jr., who had been involved in marketing with Robert Noyce at both Fairchild Semiconductor and Intel Corporation.

Jobs, Wozniak, and Markkula were bright enough to undertake some marketing research. What was the potential of the personal computer market? Would the Apple sell better as a kit or as a "turn-key" system? What was the best way to sell it? What was the price range they should aim for? Based on the answers they got, the three men developed their basic plans for capital requirements, management expertise, production facilities, software support, and marketing.

Mike Markkula put some money into Apple Computer and got together with various venture capitalists, including Venrock Associates and the man who put Intel Corporation (and others) into business, Arthur Rock.

The Apple computer became one of the most popular products of the late 1970s and early 1980s. Thousands of them were sold. Because the company did its marketing properly and had a technologically simple product (in comparison with what was available), they not only satisfied the growing market made up of computer buffs, but created whole new markets where none had existed before. By 1983, Apple Computer had grown from two men working in a garage to an international corporation of four thousand people with annual sales of more than a *billion* dollars. In the same year, Apple Computer became the youngest company ever to enter the ranks of the Fortune 500. Taking inflation and the buying power of the dollar into account, Apple Computer didn't make it any bigger than Fairchild, Intel, Hewlett-Packard, or even Texas Instruments. But they did it in less time.

The company went public in December 1980 with an initial offering of 4.6 million shares of common stock. In May 1981, there was a secondary offering of 2.6 million shares from about a hundred stockholders who had acquired their shares through employee stock plans or private placement. Both Jobs and Wozniak became the modern embodiments of the Great American Entrepreneurial Dream. Suddenly, both of them were worth millions of dollars.

Steve Jobs owns the obligatory Mercedes, but prefers to ride his motorcycle. Friends say he hasn't changed much, but several million dollars can and does change anyone a little bit. Steve Wozniak has gained more than a little notoriety for bankrolling large rock concerts in southern California; they don't make any money, but they don't have to.

And all Jobs, Wozniak, and Markkula had done was to take existing computer hardware and software, put it together to satisfy a market they knew was there, and sell it not only to the computer buffs who had wanted it, but to millions of others who didn't know they wanted it in 1976.

Computer Dealer magazine said of them in January 1983:

"No one manufacturer has had a greater impact on the personal computer market than Apple Computer." Impact? Apple Computer practically *created* the market!

"No company has done more than Apple to dispel the notion that computers are inscrutible beasts," said *Fortune* in February 1983.

"In the lasting tradition of the American Dream, the firm has made a better machine at lower cost. Wouldn't it be great if GM, Ford, or Chrysler could do the same thing for cars?" asked *Popular Computing* in March 1983. GM, Ford, and Chrysler had already done it fifty years before; with the automotive industry in its robust maturity, the Ford Model T wouldn't sell in 1983.

And, as in the automotive industry when Ford showed the way toward the popular automobile, Apple Computer bred its own competition as well as shocking every other large computer manufacturer into catering to this huge new market.

17

The Computer Becomes Competitive

It may surprise people to learn that the "big" computer companies such as IBM, NCR, Honeywell, and DEC didn't spot the emergence of the personal computer in the form of the Jobs-Wozniak Apple. The computer buffs working in these companies certainly did, because many of Apple's initial customers were people who already knew something about computers. They undoubtedly brought the Apple to the attention of their supervisors and managers, and from there the news spread to the marketing departments of these huge companies.

If there is one thing that the history of the computer reveals it is that the evaluations of the marketing department usually are incorrect on the conservative side.

In 1976, the big main-frame computer companies may have viewed the personal computer as having a limited market because their engineers *knew* how expensive it was to produce a computer and its peripherals. They also sensed that although the hardware could be produced at a reasonably high rate like Japanese transistor radios—production is a matter of more and bigger of the same in which one must order in larger quantities, hire more people, and lease a bigger plant—their programmers *knew* that the development of the program software wasn't up to the awesome task of putting the complicated computer into the

193

hands of anyone except a computer expert or computer buff.

However, just as the electronic circuit engineers over-looked the fact that their profession was becoming moribund with the development of IC chips, so the programmers failed to see that once a program is written and debugged, it would run forever. True, new machines and new operating systems require a continual improvement and customization of software. But one there are enough machines out there, the good programs become the standard programs, and new ones aren't needed because computer designers make hardware that's compatible with the ubiquitous software. Who has to program in machine language anymore?

But all of this seems to have been beyond most of the main-frame computer companies in the mid-1970s.

So it wasn't the big main-frame computer companies with their enormous storehouses of expertise that jumped in to follow Apple. The competition came from two other sources: consumer electronics companies that weren't into computers yet and were looking to expand their consumer markets, and other people like Jobs and Wozniak, the good old American entrepreneurs starting companies in their garages. There were several of the first and thousands of the latter, so many that it's impossible to consider each of them. But examples of each can be selected to provide a general idea of what was going on and how it was done.

Charles Tandy didn't pay a penny for Radio Shack Corpora-tion when he bought it in April 1963. The company had started in 1921 as an electronic parts supply store in New England. By 1950, it had grown to be one of the Big Four in its field—consumer sales of equipment and parts through chains of franchised stores and by direct mail. The others were Allied Radio, Lafayette Electronics, and Burstein-Applebee. By 1963 Radio Shack had developed its own brand names—Realistic® and Archer® among them—in order to undersell the established brands. So had Allied, Lafayette, and B-A. The reasons behind this are simple to one knowledgeable in retailing. If "the Shack" sold RCA radio tubes, it was competing against every other RCA dealer. But if they got RCA to produce a large run of vacuum tubes for Radio Shack with the Realistic® name on them, Radio Shack could buy the tubes at quantity prices and sell them at low retail prices while preserving the high profit margin they had to maintain because of huge inventories of forty thousand or more items stocked in each retail store to satisfy the consumer demand of the time, and the high printing, mailing, and advertising costs involved in direct mail merchandising.

But in 1963, Radio Shack and every one of the Big Four was in trouble. The number of electronic components—transistors especially—had proliferated beyond all imagining. Furthermore, individual part costs had dropped fantastically. When an individual transistor retails at a dollar or less, and there are thousands of them that must be stocked, a *lot* of transistors have to be sold even if you keep 60 percent of the retail price as gross profit. Add to this the fact that the electronic engineers had been improving quality control all along, resulting in parts that last longer, and it leads to the fact that consumers don't come through the door as often to replace tubes or transistors. On top of this, Radio Shack was competing against itself with its own line of built-up electronic, hi-fi, and stereo equipment; people didn't want to spend the time and effort building a stereo preamplifier using a circuit diagram and individual parts when they could buy the same thing for about the same price along with a warranty to boot.

The consumer electronics business had become unprofitable by 1963 primarily because of the way in which the businesses in it were being run and because the companies were still marketing their product as though their customers were 100 percent electronics buffs and radio hams. Maybe some general managers saw that a change in marketing strategy had to be developed, but they were too broke to implement such a thing.

The First National Bank of Boston had loaned Radio Shack $7 million, and the bank wanted to be paid back eventually. When it became clear that Radio Shack's balance sheet was teetering precariously on the edge of bankruptcy, First National Bank of Boston's chairman, William L. Brown, tried to sell the company to Allied and Lafayette. But those companies were also faltering for the same reasons. Then Brown thought of Charles Tandy, who was looking for a consumer electronics company to supplement five electronics stores he owned in Texas.

Charles Tandy, an entrepreneur in the grand American tradition, grew up in Fort Worth, Texas, the son of a partner in the Hinckley-Tandy Leather Company, supplier of soles and shoe repair equipment. Tandy bought leather strips from his father for a penny each, sold them to schoolmates for a nickel each, and taught his customers how to fashion leather belts. His customers came away with a leather belt that was worth far more than a nickel, and they helped Charles Tandy make money. Fifty years later, Charles Tandy had taken over his father's company and built it into a huge NYSE-listed billion-dollar conglomerate involved in everything from floor tile to needlepoint and imports to flashlight batteries.

When Tandy bought Radio Shack on April 4, 1963, the company was indeed bankrupt, but nobody knew it. Tandy had agreed to buy it for what it was worth, but nobody knew what that figure was. By the time the auditors found out that Radio Shack was a mere $1.5 million short, Tandy had signed the papers and the bankers were pleased that they'd gotten some-one substantial to cover the $7 million loan. When Radio Shack turned out to be worthless, Tandy smiled, too, and put away his checkbook. He'd gotten a bargain, and he knew it. He'd been ready to pay a considerable sum because he wanted Radio Shack to supplement his five Texas electronics stores. He was driven by the concept that electronics could be a novel and educational leisure-time activity, and he worked hard to find ways for other people to thus spend their leisure time and money.

When the bankers asked Tandy what kind of a manage-ment team he planned to bring in, the 6-foot 220-pound Texan took his Corona Belvedere cigar out of his mouth and said: "Team? What team? I'm the team." He began flying up to Boston every weekend to work on the business. He met with groups of people in the company for long hours trying to find out who was doing what, where the company saw itself, and what its place in the market was. A few weeks later, he showed up in Boston with a reorganization plan. It was scrawled on the back of an American Airlines ticket envelope. He'd figured out the product line, the merchandising approach, and the number of buyers and engineers who would be required. On the back of that envelope, Tandy had sketched ideas that unlocked the consumer electronics market where others had failed. Radio Shack still operates that way today.

Tandy wanted to have thousands of small stores all across

the nation where people could come and shop. People snickered when he said he'd open five hundred stores. But by 1982, Radio Shack had more than eighty-five hundred stores around the world.

Tandy changed the image and inventory of the stores. They became slick retail outlets able to stand on their own in the fanciest shopping malls. He pared the product line from forty thousand items to about twenty-six hundred, bagged or boxed every item, and required every store to carry the complete line. He established a pricing policy that undercut other retailers' prices while managing to keep 59 percent of every sales dollar.

Charles Tandy believed in individual incentive, and one of the first management policies he put into effect in Radio Shack was an employee performance merit award system of money or stock.

He was fond of direct mail sales and began to spend up to 9 percent of Tandy's revenues on advertising and direct mail. Most companies spend 4 percent. "Your best customer is always the person you just sold something to," Tandy believed. Even today, a Radio Shack salesperson gets your name and address on the sales slip, even for a fifty-cent battery, and that data is fed into the Radio Shack mailing list, the biggest in the nation.

Radio Shack grew so quickly that in 1975 its sales eclipsed those of its parent company, the Tandy Corporation. This is a rare event in the business world. Most Wall Street analysts thought of Tandy as Radio Shack. So, in 1975, Charles Tandy spun off everything but Radio Shack, keeping only the family heirloom leather goods divisions as Tandy Brands and the craft and home decorating divisions as Tandycrafts.

In 1967, Charles Tindall, then vice-president and treasurer of Tandy Corporation, heard of a bright young man working as the data-processing manager for a local consumer finance company. Tandy itself was computerizing and needed someone to run those operations. So he hired John Vinson Roach, a graduate of Texas Christian University with degrees in engineering and business. Tindall recalled: "Mr. Tandy would go out and buy a company on a weekend, and John was responsible for taking over its data processing on Monday morning." In setting up the computer programs for the rapidly expanding conglomerate, Roach got to know Tandy Corporation from the inside. He did a good job. First he was promoted to head of warehousing, then he became vice-president in charge of manufacturing at Radio Shack's twenty plants in North America and the Orient.

John Roach, as a computer expert, knew what was going on in Silicon Valley in faraway California. He saw Intel's micro-processor come along. He knew from Radio Shack's own sales of IC and computer chips that the personal computer market was out there. He talked Charles Tandy into letting him develop a personal computer for Radio Shack. And he was not very far behind Jobs and Wozniak.

In 1977, Radio Shack introduced the TRS-80™ Model I. It consisted of a keypad, a display terminal, and a cassette re-corder for prerecorded programs and storing data. As computers go today, the TRS-80™ Model I was what the computer buffs call a "kluge." It had only 4K of internal working memory, which meant that a customer really couldn't do very much with it except play some simple games. It was a very primitive personal computer. It was designed with cost and price in mind. (The first TRS-80™ Model I units with 4K RAM eventually sold for $499.) It used a unique and unusual operating system that wasn't compatible with any other computer, but it was cheap and it worked. And it was targeted toward a market above and beyond the computer buff: the Radio Shack consumer who walked through the doors of thousands of Radio Shack stores to buy CB gear, radio ham equipment, and stereo components. The computer buffs didn't like the TRS-80™. In fact, many of them have no kind words for it even today when it and its progeny have become among the biggest selling personal com-puters in the world. The buffs call it the "Trash-Eighty." They don't like it because of its operating system and the fact that this system means it has to be programmed a little differently than any other personal computer.

Four years after the TRS-80™ came to market, thousands had been sold, making it competitive in popularity with the Apple, the Commodore, and the other personal computers that had flooded the market by 1981. Radio Shack split the computer sales operation off from its electronic equipment and parts stores, establishing more than twelve hundred Radio Shack Computer Centers in the larger metropolitan areas. However, each Radio Shack store still sells TRS-80s™ and all the peripherals, software, and other goodies that have been developed in the intervening years.

Radio Shack pioneered something else: "user friendly" salesmen. One of the big problems with buying a personal computer in the 1976-83 time period was the fact that the little computer shops that sprang up around the country to peddle the Apples, Commodores, Vics, Ataris, Cromencos, North Stars, and their ilk had been founded by computer engineers, computer marketing people, data-processing experts, and computer buffs. Computer technology created its own language, one full of acronyms that became nouns, verbs, adjectives, and adverbs. It used new words that had been invented to describe computer hardware, software, and operations. It took old words and gave them new meanings. It developed conglomerate words. Computer store salesmen had a tendency to speak to their customers as though the customers were buffs themselves. They used "computerese" to hype the features of their products. The sales pitch would be full of bits, bytes, bauds, access times, bootstraps, algorithms, buffers, firmware, parity, handshaking, and strings. Such a computer salesman was once humorously referred to as "human-friendly liveware." This sort of thing drove away more customers than it created and further fueled the erroneous concept that computers were alien invaders unable to communicate with people. On the other hand, Radio Shack trained their salesmen to speak English. It helped immensely.

Radio Shack kept right on improving the TRS-80™. Today its operating system is compatible or can be made compatible with every other computer system by means of an "interface" module. In 1984, they introduced the TRS-80™ Model 100, a battery-operated book-size personal computer with a liquid crystal display screen, built-in modem for direct connection to phone lines, and five built-in programs for word processing, data base, and BASIC.

In 1983, Tandy Radio Shack was rated the nineteenth largest computer company in the world with sales in excess of $2.4 billion dollars, almost 35 percent of which was from computer hardware and software sales. John Vinson Roach, the man who had brought Radio Shack into the computer business, had become chairman of the board, chief executive officer, and president.

In the second category of companies that set out to produce personal computers is one that is an unusual example of enterprise because it was founded by and is still managed by two suburban housewives.

In 1976, Lore Harp knew nothing at all about computers and very little about business. Born and brought up in a small village near Dusseldorf, West Germany, Lore's father was a businessman and her grandfather had been a highly successful politician in the Weimar Republic prior to Adolph Hitler's rise to power. She grew up with the attitude that success was achievable. She came to the United States in 1966 on a sightseeing trip to visit some friends before going on to college in Germany. When she got here, she decided to see if she could do something on her own. After spending the planned few months with a family in Santa Cruz, California, she decided she wasn't ready to go home to Germany. So she sold the return-trip part of her airline ticket and moved to San Francisco. Her parents tried to get her to come home by not sending her money, hoping to starve her out.

"I just wanted to see what else there was," Harp told Eliza G. C. Collins of *Harvard Business Review*. "All the people I had met and stayed with were white, Republican, and wealthy. This was 1966, and so many other things were going on that I wanted to experience. I wasn't running away, though. I never got into a drug culture or anything of that nature; I was just terribly curious about life and what makes people tick. I had so much time ahead of me that it didn't seem a few more months out of my life would make that big a difference to what I did. I only had a visitor's visa, so I could neither go to school nor officially work. So I did all sorts of little diddly things, like babysitting. At one point I was down to twenty dollars, but I just would not call my parents and ask them to send me any money. Somehow I always made it. I had nothing to fall back on, but I suppose I knew that if things got too tough I could call my parents and have them send me a ticket."

She stayed a year and was ready to go home when she met Dr. Robert S. Harp, who was then working on his Ph.D. in electrical engineering at Stanford University. She decided to go to school in California and get her bachelor's degree in anthropology. She married Bob Harp, and they had two daughters. Lore entered law school when the family moved to Westlake

Village, California, and Bob went to work as a senior scientist at Hughes Aircraft's research center in nearby Malibu. But the reading required too much of her time. Lore wasn't happy as a housewife, though. She couldn't stand being at home and she couldn't get herself involved in PTA and volunteer work with the other suburban housewives.

She found a friend in Carole Ely, a New Jerseyite and Cornell graduate who'd worked in financial and portfolio management with the Ford Foundation and Merrill Lynch. Carole had come west with her husband and two children when her husband was offered a career opportunity. The two housewives met because their respective children were in the same school. Both women were restless, and both were looking for achievement of some sort. They toyed with the idea of setting up a travel agency.

Bob Harp had designed a computer memory board and had arranged to have it marketed through another firm, but something happened and the whole deal fell through. He knew that Lore was restless, so in 1976 he asked her if she'd like to set up a little company and market his memory board. Lore thought it sounded fantastic, but she didn't know anything about business. Her friend Carole did. The two of them got together over the Harp kitchen table and decided that even though neither of them knew a bit from a byte, they'd try it.

Two days later, the two housewives drove down to a Southern California Computer Society trade show to check out the market.

"I was absolutely overwhelmed," Lore Harp admits. "The computer hobbyists were the weirdest people I'd ever met. They were very enthused about computers and very, very bright, but they could hardly get a word out. Then they would peel off eight hundred, nine hundred, or a thousand dollars in cash to buy a few memory boards. And I thought, 'My God, there must be a tremendous market.' But the stuff looked so tacky."

Harp and Ely figured they'd be able to sell a few thousand dollars worth of memory boards. So they got together $6,000, formed a California corporation they called Vector Graphic, Inc., hired an accountant to set up the books, arranged for the corporation to pay Bob Harp a 5 percent royalty on boards he designed (he elected to remain at Hughes just in case Vector Graphic wasn't a success), and turned a downstairs bedroom-bathroom suite into an office-factory-warehouse. They kept their supply of plastic packing popcorn in the shower stall. Lore and Carole began working from 9:00 A.M. to 10:00 P.M. every day. Salesmen from various vendors would call on the company in the sedate house in suburban Westlake Village. Off and on throughout the day, these men would arrive and then leave about an hour later. Lore Harp remarked: "The neighbors must have thought we have a very successful little brothel going!"

Lore and Carole decided they'd have to both create a good image and get exposure for it. They placed half-page and full-page ads in trade publications. They got a well-designed corporate logo and used high-quality linen bond stationery. Their shipping boxes were printed in green and white with their logo prominent on all sides. This modern marketing approach took the computer hobbyists by storm. "They used to call us 'the girls in green and white,' " Lore recalled.

On their quality stationery, they sent a letter to every dealer listed in the ads of competing memory board manufacturers. The letter began, "Dear Dealer: Meet the Vector 8K baby." They called it that because Bob Harp had designed it to plug into a mother board, computer terminology for the main structure. A week after they mailed the letters, they followed up with a personal telephone call to each dealer, asking them how many memory boards they wanted to buy. Usually, a dealer would order just one. Then, the women would call the dealers back in a week or so and ask how they liked the board and if there was anything else they could do to help them sell more of them.

None of the boards was ever returned. The dealers fell all over one another. They'd never been treated so well. None of the other small manufacturers of computer hobbyist hardware did things like that. This, in turn, flabbergasted Lore and Carole. "We just couldn't imagine selling any other way," Lore remarked. On November 30, 1976, Lore and Carole sold eighty-one memory boards at $150 each, a gross of $12,150 in one day. Sales just kept going up from there.

Looking back on it, the reasons are simple. The two women had a natural understanding of the modern principles of mass distribution. They supported their sales effort with the sort of service that was exceedingly rare in the infant personal computer business. They shipped on time. They provided good manuals. They didn't mind sending documentation such as drawings and circuit schematics. They did trouble-shooting over the telephone with customers, and when they couldn't answer a question, they called Bob Harp at Hughes.

Dr. Bob Harp, who had to contend with equipment compatibility problems every day in the research laboratory, decided to standardize the design of the Vector Graphic computer boards and eventually all of the products around what is known as the "S-100 bus." This was developed by the computer buffs as a standardized way of lining up and connecting the multiple-pin sockets into which the computer boards where inserted. Any board designed and built to use the S-100 bus could be plugged into any computer using this standard. The big companies were trying to ignore the S-100 bus in those days. Managers, marketing men, and even engineers tend to want to design products in a nonstandard, exclusive way so that their equipment and only their equipment will work in their products, thus locking in the customer. It doesn't work very long because sooner or later one way of doing things becomes standardized for design, production, or maintenance convenience, and there has never been a technical hobbyist or amateur born who can't figure out a way to beat this "exclusivity game."

Standardization was a brilliant technical decision on Bob Harp's part and did much to foster the acceptance of Vector Graphic products.

In 1977, the personal computer industry began to move very fast with Apple, Commodore, and Radio Shack. Wall Street began to get excited about the "home computer market." Lore and Carole, running a small company, had the ability to move quickly and change direction fast. On the advice of Bob Harp, they decided that Vector Graphic would go after the small business market between the expensive Wangs, Laniers, and NCRs and the less rugged, versatile, powerful, and expensive Apples and Commodores. This was also a good decision because, when the economy began to turn down, firms didn't have money to spend for the expensive business machines and people couldn't lay out several thousand dollars for what was then perceived as a toy.

The Harps and Carole Ely also did something technically interesting with their new complete small computer systems: they put together a neat package of compact hardware, the Vector Graphic I of 1977, followed in 1979 by the Vector Graphic

System B with built-in high-density diskette drives. Each featured hardware designed around software programs tailored
specifically to the system. This permitted Vector Graphic systems to have versatile and powerful programs for word processing, mailing lists, a special but compatible version of the universal BASIC language, a disk operating system (MDOS) that was
one of the first in the industry, and a compatibility with what
was then beginning to become a universal operating system,
CP/M. Furthermore, these programs were simple to operate,
some of the first "user-friendly software."

What they had the customers liked, and they'd identified
their customers and the customers' desires properly. Originally
Lore and Carole had targeted a goal of $30,000 per month in
sales; they reached that three months after shipping their first
memory board. In 1977, Bob Harp left Hughes and joined the
firm full-time. In 1978, sales were a cool $2 million, tripling to
$6 million the following year. By 1980, Vector Graphic had far
outgrown the Harps' downstairs bedroom. They moved to forty
thousand square feet of space in a Westlake Village industrial
park, where two hundred employees go to work in an unusual
industrial environment. Whenever a large order was received, a
cow bell was rung. Lore Harp and Carole Ely became a business
and management phenomenon overnight, or so it seemed. In
1980, Vector Graphic posted sales of $15 million.

Tandy Radio Shack got into the personal computer business through one door; Vector Graphic got in through another.
So did hundreds of other companies, big and small. There
seemed to be no end to the bonanza.

Then came 1981.

18

Boom, Bust, Shake-out, and "Excelsior!"

The big, established computer companies like IBM, NCR, Burroughs, Honeywell, Hewlett-Packard, Sperry, and DEC had been watching the personal computer phenomenon even though they didn't jump into it immediately. But when they did, they made a big splash.

One bright morning in August 1981, the high-roller, fast-growing, free-wheeling, entrepreneurial darling of Wall Street, the personal computer industry, woke up to discover that there were indeed giants on the earth. Furthermore, one of the Big Boys was climbing over the fences around the backyards of every small personal and business computer company.

Suddenly, it was hardball time.

The personal computer industry had been warily glancing in the direction of Armonk, New York. Industry soothsayers had been predicting that IBM was working on a personal computer. In some circles, this was greeted with derisive laughter. Such a move on IBM's part would mean that "Big Blue" would have to change corporate policies and adopt new marketing philosophies far removed from those that had served it so well since the firm was conglomerated as the C-T-R Company by banker Charles R. Flint in 1911. IBM couldn't change seventy years of established procedures overnight.

But it happened. International Business Machines announced the IBM 5150 PC Personal Computer several months before anyone thought it would. But IBM did more than that. It had previously clung tenaciously to such proprietary items as systems specifications and had strictly controlled the development of software from non-IBM sources. Now they released the full nine yards of their PC specifications and opened the doors to all comers who wanted to develop software for it.

To add insult to injury insofar as the small personal computer industry was concerned, IBM announced that it would not only rely on its own well-trained, Watson-inspired in-house sales force for the PC, as it had done for everything else it produced, but it would expand its sales base by allowing the IBM PC to be sold in computer shops such as Computerland and huge retail outlets such as Sears, Roebuck and Company.

The small computer industry knew that IBM could and would mount a massive advertising campaign behind this new product, utilizing television and all the other mass media. IBM could afford it. A few others could try, but nobody could hope to beat "Big Blue," much less even equal it, in this area.

When it appeared in the spring of 1982, the IBM PC wasn't cheap. It didn't try to compete on price with Apple, Commodore, Atari, TRS-80™ and the rest. The feeling in the industry was mixed because those who managed to get their hands on some of the first IBM PCs to hit the market quickly concluded that much of the higher price was simply because of the IBM label on the front of the machine.

Furthermore, when the computer engineers and buffs got into the IBM PC to analyze it, they discovered that it had been very cleverly overdesigned in such a way that IBM could (and did) come back in a few years to offer an update to increase speed, memory, or computational power. IBM was counting on customer loyalty. The company knew that thousands of businesses, big and small, throughout the world had bought IBM electric and Selectric typewriters, and many of them had bought and used various IBM computers down through the years. "Big Blue" IBM, like "Jimmy" GM and "Generous" Electric, was a company that could be counted on to be Big Daddy and take care of its customers.

Some companies fervently believed that IBM might at last have bitten off more than it could chew. But that wasn't the case. Within one year, IBM had captured 17 percent of the microcomputer market—personal and small business. By the end of 1983, it had 23 percent of it.

Fortunately, the small computer business doesn't represent a finite pie in which IBM's 23 percent slice means there's that much less to be divided up between everyone else. If there's one thing computer history has shown us, it's that its market is a rapidly (almost exponentially) growing pie. The big question in 1981-82 was: will the pie continue to grow fast enough to accommodate IBM's increasing share of it, along with an increasing share for everyone else, too?

IBM's entry also indicated something else had happened that few people recognized: computer technology reached a definite plateau in the 1970s. The hardware was well established by 1981. It could do just about anything most people reasonably wanted it to do. Computers were so fast they seemed to work almost instantaneously; an increase in speed was of interest only to a few people who were working on very complex and esoteric problems in science and economics. Were 16-bit microprocessors really worth a new machine in comparison to what could be done with an 8-bit computer? Working memories of 64K or 128K were large enough for most small and personal computer applications, especially if floppy disks or Winchester hard disks could be used to provide additional memory when data wasn't immediately required in the program. Why update to 128K or 256K working memory if 48K or 64K RAM was adequate? Floppy disks and diskettes were adequate storage media, although the three-inch "microfloppies" began to make their appearance in 1983. Color displays and graphics had reached a high plateau of adequacy although there was still an interest in replacing the bulky cathode-ray tube display with a solid-state flat display. With the modem, a relatively inexpensive piece of electronics, any computer could be hooked into the ubiquitous telephone communications network of North America (or the world) and talk to other computers, big and small, to increase computer power or simply to communicate data. Printers were still piles of mechanical buffoonery, upgraded electric typewriters in concept, but at 750 word per minute for letter-quality copy and even 1,500 words per minute for high-density dot-matrix copy, this was adequate speed for most users. (Get rid of the mechanical movements at a reasonable price, people said, and you'd have a saleable item; but, in the meantime, for the price, we'll live with the chatterboxes.) The computer buffs will always want more technology, but the consumer may be satisfied with a lot less if it does what is wanted.

In short, the computer as a piece of consumer hardware had matured in the 1970s. The next big breakthrough may be waiting in the wings, but maybe not. Maybe the market desires have been satisfied, and any futher improvement during the next decade or so would be viewed by customers as "planned obsolescence" or gimmickry for the sake of gimmickry.

Software (programs) suddenly became the hot technology items of the 1980s. But programming is a highly specialized field. Universal programs that will run on any machine depend upon the standardization of operating systems. There are several "standards" available today, all of them mutually incompatible. CP/M had grown to be probably the most ubiquitous. There are at least thirty other operating systems in use, including MS-DOS, XENIX, FLEX, BASIC, PICK, OASIS, RTTS, LEXS, MPS-10, RSX-11M, and the new Department of Defense Ada.

But the impact of the IBM PC has been so great and "Big Blue" has been so powerful that most computers in the mid-1980s are being advertised as "IBM compatible" or "capable of running IBM software."

The game changed in the 1980s. Those that recognized it survived the consequences of IBM's move and the great recession of 1978-83.

The name of the new game is "Marketing, Merchandising, and Maintenance," not the "Bits, Bytes, and Bauds" game of technology. Every computer company—Hollerith's Electric Tabulating Company, Watson's early IBM, Burroughs, Patterson's NCR, Eckert and Mauchly's UNIVAC, Intel, Apple Computer, Vector Graphic—unconsciously played this game better and better as the years went by and as the technology became more refined, requiring better marketing to know how to design the product, merchandising to sell the product, and maintenance to repair the product in the field. Every other industry based on the high technology of its time has also discovered itself playing the "MM&M" game at some point during its development. The industries established to produce automobiles, radio, television, aviation, and biologicals reached this cusp earlier in the twentieth century. In the 1980s, the computer industry discovered that "MM&M" was the big game. If you didn't play it, the history of both the computer industry and other industries showed that you'd probably fold in five to ten years. Probably less in the fast-moving computer industry.

And it's a game of hardball indeed. Some companies were equipped to play and others were not or weren't willing to. The ones who were not fell by the wayside daily.

General Electric may have seen this coming, giving them a quiet reason to opt out and sell their computer operation to Honeywell in 1971.

As of this writing, no company in the computer industry has failed in a big enough way to cause shock waves in the industry. But between 1981 and 1984, a lot of computer company executives were coming into the plant every morning and thinking to themselves: "Everyone here is depending upon me for their paycheck, and I'd better not screw up today."

One big, established firm discovered it couldn't compete in the small computer market. Texas Instruments, Inc., was and still is a powerhouse in the solid-state electronics industry. One of their people, Jack Kilby, was the coinventor of the integrated circuit chip. TI developed some outstanding pocket calculators and has retained its leadership in that market in spite of strong competition from the Orient. But when it came out with its TI 99/4A personal computer in 1981, the machine had several strikes against it from the start. It used a strange, unique operating system called DX-10. As such, it was not a derated main-frame computer like Apple, Commodore, Atari, and the rest, but an uprated pocket calculator. It was practically impossible to make it compatible with other personal computers for networking or programming. Programs that would run on the TI wouldn't run on anything else. Furthermore, it used a plug-in solid-state memory system totally unlike any other computer. The initial price was $1,500. Even when TI kept reducing the price, they and their retailers had trouble selling the machine. In 1983, TI called it quits and withdrew from the personal computer market. However, TI did *not* fail; it was too well diversified in the solid-state electronics business for that to happen.

The IBM move triggered other companies, some of them in somewhat different industries, to take a similar plunge. Among these was Coleco Industries, Inc., in West Hartford, Connecticut. Primarily a maker of toys and games, Coleco was led into the computer business by way of video games. They'd seen the toy giant, Mattel, take a bath in video games, but Coleco decided it would do things differently. As the video games became more complex, various bits of computer technology such as microprocessors and memory chips began to be integrated into the hardware, and the software required to run the games began to resemble comparable computer graphics software. In fact, video game technology requirements pushed the state of the art in computer graphics in a strange sort of synergy.

In June 1983, Coleco jumped right into the middle of the highly competitive personal computer market by announcing the ADAM. Its price was ridiculously low (about $700 or less if purchased in some discount toy stores) in comparison to other personal computers of similar capabilities, especially since ADAM came with a letter-quality printer. A standard TV set could be hooked up as a monitor, betraying Coleco's experience in video gaming. But ADAM is not a toy. It is indeed a full computer with 80K RAM, a 75-key keypad, a built-in word-processing program, a fast cassette storage deck, and a 9½-inch daisy wheel bidirectional printer with a multistrike carbon ribbon capable of 120 words per minute. It shows evidence of exceptionally good engineering, an absolute requirement for any product where price is the primary marketing element.

ADAM shook the computer industry, although not quite to the extent the IBM PC did. But ADAM had troubles. Coleco was apparently unused to the high level of quality control demanded in the computer industry, and many of the ADAM computers produced in the first few months simply wouldn't work and had to be shipped back. Coleco rectified this shortcoming, but was then forced to live down a poor starting image. Coleco contracted with Honeywell to provide customer repair and maintenance, thus helping the situation by offering quick and nearby service. With their basic toy industry orientation, the next problem they ran into was poor customer support in making available tape cassettes and printer ribbons, both of which are unique and exclusive to the ADAM. As of mid-1984, Coleco has yet to learn that many people will buy the ADAM not as an expensive computer gaming machine (an area in which ADAM and the earlier Coleco computer games compete with Atari), but as a true home computer. And home computers use up tape, printer ribbons, and paper in enormous quantities as people become familiar with the various ways in which an inexpensive but powerful machine like the ADAM can be used.

ADAM is no IBM PC, nor was it intended as such. Coleco decided to exploit a portion of the market that seemed to have been ignored by others, including Apple Computer, which abdicated its position as the inexpensive personal computer maker.

Apple Computer reacted to the IBM entry by upgrading its product line. By 1982, Apple was on the Fortune 500 list. Mike Markkula took over as president and chief executive officer in March 1981. Steve Jobs remained as chairman of the board and didn't take as much of an active role in the business as he had, preferring to drive his motorcycle and go to friends' homes to "sit around and drink wine and talk about what we're going to do when we grow up." The Apple II computer was introduced as a low-cost personal computer for small business, educational, scientific, and home use. Three quarters of a million of them were sold, when Apple Computer brought along the Apple IIe with technological innovations and the ability to run all of the Apple II software—and there was a lot of that available. The price was $1,395, competitive with the IBM PC. The Apple III used 32-bit microprocessors and touted additional speed and power for the small business and professional user. In January 1983, Lisa™ was introduced, priced "under $10,000" and using 32-bit architecture but aimed primarily at the office market. A year later, along came Macintosh, a super-Apple with all of Lisa's power and technology and priced at $2,495. To back up all this hardware in the field, Apple signed an agreement with RCA in October 1982 for on-site maintenance of Apple computers brought in to their franchised retailers. By March 1983, the company was offering extended warranty plans for all its computers through more than fourteen hundred dealers.

Apple Computer had decided to play the "MM&M" game in earnest, having apparently seen some of the consequences of the main shift in emphasis from technology to marketing in the industry. An indication of the rapidity with which the entire personal and small business computer industry matured between 1981 and 1984 is the simple but little noticed fact that all three Apple creators—Jobs, Wozniak, and Markkula—were no longer directly involved in the top management by the end of

1983. They'd brought in a new president and chief executive officer, John Sculley, formerly president of Pepsi-Cola Company, a professional corporate manager who had *not* come up through the executive ranks in the computer industry. Whether this infusion of external expertise into one of the computer industry's leading companies will work remains to be seen.

It didn't work with another small business computer company, Vector Graphic, Inc. In the throes of its own adolescence, the company had reached the awkward point of all entrepreneurial ventures: its rapid growth could no longer be supported by venture capitalists and retained earnings, and it had to have a much larger physical plant. On top of all this was the stormy marriage of Bob and Lore Harp.

The company went public in August 1981 with a $13 million initial stock offering. In negotiating the stock price with the underwriters, the no-nonsense businesslike side of Lore Harp came out. Among the things she insisted upon was stock options for Vector Graphic's long-time employees. The underwriters objected to this and other conditions. But she stood her ground and told them: "You have five more minutes. We must have a deal at the end of that time or else we're going to walk." When the underwriters looked shocked and began to hem and haw, Harp merely added: "Okay, that's thirty seconds gone." Because of the unemotional image that Lore Harp projected over the years, she grew to be known within the computer industry as "the Ice Maiden."

The pressures and stresses of rapid growth claimed two marriages in 1981: the Harps' and the Elys'. "It was an ego conflict," Bob Harp admits. "She wanted to do things one way; I wanted to do them another." Says Carole Ely: "I was running away from a marriage into a company." Bob Harp's departure as technical director left a vacancy in the engineering department that wasn't helped when three other design engineers also left. Vector Graphic found itself without any engineers working on its new products, which had to compete with the recently announced IBM PC.

And Vector Graphic moved into its own new plant in the summer of 1981. If there's one thing that always spells trouble for a young and growing company, it's a move into its own quarters specifically designed for its operations.

Lore Harp always knew when she needed help. She'd

called on Carole Ely to get expertise in the business side of their initial venture. As Vector Graphic reached $20 million in sales in 1982, she began looking around for experienced executives who had played key roles in helping other companies grow through that point in their development. Key people could no longer afford the time to learn on the job; things were changing too fast in the company and the industry, especially with IBM in the market. So, on May 20, 1982, she hired Frederick A. Snow as the new president and chief executive officer. Harp became chairman of the board.

Unlike Sculley at Apple, who had no computer industry background, Snow was a British electrical engineer who had directed Honeywell's operation in Great Britain and gone on to become vice-president of Honeywell Information Systems.

But Vector Graphic went into a slump. Snow pushed the new Vector 4 system into the market to compete with IBM in the summer of 1982. When he did this, sales of the old Vector 3 system collapsed, leaving $3 million in inventory. The first loss in the company's history—$1.2 million—was posted in the first quarter of 1983. The final blow came from IBM when, in March 1983, they dropped the price of the PC by 20 percent.

On April 29, 1983, Harp fired Snow "because he wasn't a street fighter," and she took over the management of the company again. Things had gone to hell in the company in just one year. Morale was shot. Discipline had disappeared. Management had generally lost control. The first meeting after Harp resumed the presidency was scheduled for 4:30 P.M. on a Friday afternoon. A large number of people were late. Harp looked around and said simply: "One of the things we need to do in order to get this company back on track is to exhibit discipline, and discipline starts with starting on time. This is the last time I'm going to see somebody late to a meeting. We don't have time for a lot of pussyfooting around." Harp didn't need to pare the fat from the personnel roles; the fat quit and went looking for other companies. She reinstituted the management practices that had made Vector Graphic both successful and a good place to work. By early 1984, the company was recovering and targeting its share of the market at 5 percent. Vector Graphic survived because Lore Harp is a survivor.

So did the rest of the industry because, strange as its people may seem to be to outsiders, the computer people turned out to be survivors like those in other high-tech industries. The strange assortment of professional managers, technically oriented engineers, computer buffs, and entrepreneurs slowly learned to play the new game in town. The sheer size of the industry in 1983 was enormous. And it kept growing daily.

Although competition became fierce with the entry of IBM, "Big Blue" didn't get the field all to itself. In fact, IBM's venture into the small computer field prompted others to get in, too, probably because of the general feeling that "if IBM can do it and not get hurt, so can we." Among the manufacturers of small personal and business computers listed by *Computerworld* in its 1983 buyer's guide (the latest available at the time of this writing), the following Big Boys are producing computers in the performance and general price range of the various models of Apple, TRS-80^{tm}, and Commodore: Data General Corporation, Digital Equipment Corporation, Fujitsu Microelectronics, Inc., Hewlett-Packard, Hitachi, IBM, Intel, Lanier Business Products, Mitsubishi Electronics America, Inc., NCR Corporation, Panasonic, Sanyo Business Systems Corporation, Toshiba America, Inc., Xerox Corporation, and Zenith Data Systems, Inc.

The entry of Japanese electronic firms into the computer market in the early 1980s created a lot of agony among American computer company executives because they remembered what had happened with the transistor radio and the automobile. But by 1984, it appeared that American technology still had the edge over Japanese production capability. The Japanese have finally come up against a segment of American industry that is perhaps managed as well, if not better, than the Japanese manage their own firms. Certainly the management tone in such companies as Apple, Intel, and Vector Graphic is nothing like the Japanese have encountered before.

The history of technology in other high-tech areas—aviation, rocketry, and radar, for example—has shown one particular American characteristic with stark clarity: American industry may or may not be first in a given technical area, but when American high-tech industrialists gain a full understanding of their markets, there is no one in the world who can match them. The Wright brothers invented the modern airplane, the Europeans built the first airlines and airliners, but it was the Douglas DC-3 that made airlines everywhere profitable and the DC-4 that made the European flying boats obsolete and opened the transoceanic airlanes. It was the Italian Marchese Guglielmo Marconi who developed the first practical wireless radio systems, but American entrepreneurs and technologists made radio and television a practical success. Robert H. Goddard built the first liquid propellant rockets in Massachusetts, the Germans perfected the space rocket, but it was Americans who landed on the moon. The automobile was invented by Daimler and Benz in Germany, but perfected in its present form in the United States; the recent phenomenon of Japanese automotive supremacy may turn out in the long run to have been an opportunistic move on the part of the Japanese.

The only proper assessment of the Japanese competitive threat that can be given at this time is the same assessment that the late historian Will Durant made when he was asked what he thought the consequences of the French Revolution were: "It's too early yet to tell." The United States of America is, after all, what Pulitzer Prize-winning historian Daniel J. Boorstin calls the "republic of technology. We remain the world's laboratory. We like to try the new as do few other peoples in the world." The United States is an "experimental civilization."

No other culture could have given birth to and nurtured such a technical revolution as we have followed in this book.

And since it seems to have happened so quickly, although it took nearly a hundred years to reach this point, even people deeply involved in it have had a tendency to lose perspective.

The computer industry is a multibillion-dollar operation.

In August 1983's *Computerworld Buyers Guide,* 415 computer manufacturers were listed.

In breaking down their products by price range, each category listed below has the indicated number of different computer systems available:

Under $5,000	330
$5,000 - $10,000	256
$10,000 - $20,000	167
$20,000 - $50,000	145
$50,000 - $100,000	79
$100,000 - $500,000	123
$500,000 - $1,000,000	21
$1,000,000 up	45

This is only the hardware made by computer hardware companies. There are even more software companies. And there are yet more companies, big and small, making subsystems such as printers, cables, disk drives, PC boards, ICs and LSIs, enclosures, and a host of other products that the OEMs (Original Equipment Manufacturers) assemble into operating computer systems. Beyond that, there are the computer supply companies selling furniture, diskettes, disks, tape, printer ribbons, terminal covers, printwheels, and paper. To maintain the millions of computers now being used, a massive network of repair and maintenance facilities has come into existence.

It would have seemed incredible to Charles Babbage. But it's just the beginning.

Epilogue

$\bigcirc$ne of the problems with a history book is that it must stop at some point in time, which is then considered "the present time." But history doesn't stop. The instant of time we call the "present" immediately becomes the "past." This is therefore only the first part of a saga whose end we cannot yet see and whose consequences we can only speculate about.

But a number of patterns have emerged, and they deserve comment.

It has often been said that "history repeats itself." This is not true. It is the patterns of history that repeat. History is made by people, and people haven't changed physiologically or psychologically for at least fifty thousand years.

People in the computer industry tend to think of themselves as unique, as did every other generation in every other high-tech field. But each succeeding generation has been better educated and has had better technology to help them work toward a long-range goal that nobody has yet attained: the full development and use of the mental capabilities of every individual human being. Computers are helping in this regard because computers have been developed by people as mental and intellectual tools. Although the nontechnical intelligentsia may continue to fear that mankind's technology is creating mankind's successor or will destroy the species, those who are involved in the computer revolution have always understood that *people* create technology and its devices for human use.

Don't ask what a computer can do that a human being cannot. Ask instead: what can a human being do that a computer cannot? The answer: a human being can do the things that a computer cannot do—and that is 99 percent of everything.

If the patterns of history repeat themselves, then we have certainly seen the development of patterns in the history of computers. It's not surprising that these same patterns also exist in the development of other areas of technology.

One of the most important of these general patterns may be more fully grasped by considering what historians Will and Ariel Durant said in their 1968 book *The Lessons of History:* "The experience of the past leaves little doubt that every economic system must sooner or later rely upon some form of profit motive to stir individuals and groups to productivity. Substitutes like slavery, police supervision, or ideological enthusiasm prove too unproductive, too expensive, or too transient. Normally and generally, men are judged by their ability to produce. . . ."

The enormous technical and social progress that has come about because of the computer is totally and completely the result of individual initiative. Governments may have bought the computers, but the computer industry, unlike the aerospace industry, isn't almost totally dependent upon government funding. And there are no bureaucratic requirements for a government permit to develop a computer, build one, or own one. We can be profoundly thankful for this. Had it happened, and had the enormous information-processing capabilities of the modern computer fallen exclusively into the hands of a strong central government, we might indeed be living in an Orwellian world. Although the power of a central government has been strengthened by the computer and, in fact, would be impossible without the computer, the fact that an individual can possess a comparable computer acts to moderate the power of large organizations over the individual.

By and large, the computer is the result of people working to better their own condition and that of their families. Some people are enamored of the technology. Others are seduced by the marketplace. And yet others simply want something interesting to do. In all cases, everybody wins.

The development of the computer is itself part of a larger historical pattern. The history of the computer has confirmed the theory that the main line of development of human civilization has always moved through those cultures in which individual enterprise has been at a premium and in which the political, economic, and other social institutions existed to encourage this. All kinds of people worked on computers, experimenting doggedly with old ideas and originating and testing new ideas, ironing the shortcomings and defects out of the computers until they had made them work the way they wanted them to and in ways that would be of value to other people. They found out how to make computers perform operations of value, and they learned how to convince other people of this. If the computers hadn't performed work of value to people, and if this hadn't been communicated, people would not have bought them. The computer people did these things because they might grow rich if they succeeded. But they were given no assurance that they wouldn't lose everything if they failed.

Many failed, and many won. And all of us won in the long term.

Although there are still those who fear the computers that people make, this history of computers should instill in us not fear and anxiety, but rather pride and hope for the human race and its future.

The computer revolution has just begun.